Crisis Management in Higher Education

Hal Hoverland, Pat McInturff,
C. E. Tapie Rohm, Jr., *Editors*
California State University, San Bernardino

NEW DIRECTIONS FOR HIGHER EDUCATION
MARTIN KRAMER, *Editor-in-Chief*
University of California, Berkeley

Number 55, Fall 1986

Paperback sourcebooks in
The Jossey-Bass Higher Education Series

Jossey-Bass Inc., Publishers
San Francisco • London

Hal Hoverland, Pat McInturff,
C. E. Tapie Rohm, Jr. (Eds.).
Crisis Management in Higher Education.
New Directions for Higher Education, no. 55.
Volume XIV, number 3.
San Francisco: Jossey-Bass, 1986.

New Directions for Higher Education
Martin Kramer, *Editor-in-Chief*

Copyright © 1986 by Jossey-Bass Inc., Publishers
and
Jossey-Bass Limited

Copyright under International, Pan American, and Universal Copyright Conventions. All rights reserved. No part of this issue may be reproduced in any form—except for brief quotation (not to exceed 500 words) in a review or professional work—without permission in writing from the publishers.

New Directions for Higher Education is published quarterly by Jossey-Bass Inc., Publishers (publication number USPS 990-880). *New Directions* is numbered sequentially—please order extra copies by sequential number. The volume and issue numbers above are included for the convenience of libraries. Second-class postage paid at San Francisco, California, and at additional mailing offices. POSTMASTER: Send address changes to Jossey-Bass Inc., Publishers, 433 California Street, San Francisco, California 94104.

Editorial correspondence should be sent to the Editor-in-Chief, Martin Kramer, 2807 Shasta Road, Berkeley, California 94708.

Library of Congress Catalog Card Number 85-81888

International Standard Serial Number ISSN 0271-0560

International Standard Book Number ISBN 1-55542-984-X

Cover art by WILLI BAUM

Manufactured in the United States of America

Ordering Information

The paperback sourcebooks listed below are published quarterly and can be ordered either by subscription or single-copy.
Subscriptions cost $40.00 per year for institutions, agencies, and libraries. Individuals can subscribe at the special rate of $30.00 per year *if payment is by personal check*. (Note that the full rate of $40.00 applies if payment is by institutional check, even if the subscription is designated for an individual.) Standing orders are accepted.
Single copies are available at $9.95 when payment accompanies order, and *all single-copy orders under $25.00 must include payment*. (California, New Jersey, New York, and Washington, D.C., residents please include appropriate sales tax.) For billed orders, cost per copy is $9.95 plus postage and handling. (Prices subject to change without notice.)
Bulk orders (ten or more copies) of any individual sourcebook are available at the following discounted prices: 10-49 copies, $8.95 each; 50-100 copies, $7.96 each; over 100 copies, *inquire*. Sales tax and postage and handling charges apply as for single copy orders.
Please note that these prices are for the academic year 1986-1987 and are subject to change without prior notice. Also, some titles may be out of print and therefore not available for use.
To ensure correct and prompt delivery, all orders must give either the *name of an individual* or an *official purchase order number*. Please submit your order as follows:

Subscriptions: specify series and year subscription is to begin.
Single Copies: specify sourcebook code (such as, HE1) and first two words of title.

Mail orders for United States and Possessions, Latin America, Canada, Japan, Australia, and New Zealand to:
    Jossey-Bass Inc., Publishers
    433 California Street
    San Francisco, California 94104

Mail orders for all other parts of the world to:
    Jossey-Bass Limited
    28 Banner Street
    London EC1Y 8QE

New Directions for Higher Education Series
Martin Kramer, *Editor-in-Chief*

HE1   *Facilitating Faculty Development,* Mervin Freedman
HE2   *Strategies for Budgeting,* George Kaludis
HE3   *Services for Students,* Joseph Katz

HE4 Evaluating Learning and Teaching, C. Robert Pace
HE5 Encountering the Unionized University, Jack H. Schuster
HE6 Implementing Field Experience Education, John Duley
HE7 Avoiding Conflict in Faculty Personnel Practices, Richard Peairs
HE8 Improving Statewide Planning, James L. Wattenbarger, Louis W. Bender
HE9 Planning the Future of the Undergraduate College, Donald G. Trites
HE10 Individualizing Education by Learning Contracts, Neal R. Berte
HE11 Meeting Women's New Educational Needs, Clare Rose
HE12 Strategies for Significant Survival, Clifford T. Stewart, Thomas R. Harvey
HE13 Promoting Consumer Protection for Students, Joan S. Stark
HE14 Expanding Recurrent and Nonformal Education, David Harman
HE15 A Comprehensive Approach to Institutional Development, William Bergquist, William Shoemaker
HE16 Improving Educational Outcomes, Oscar Lenning
HE17 Renewing and Evaluating Teaching, John A. Centra
HE18 Redefining Service, Research, and Teaching, Warren Bryan Martin
HE19 Managing Turbulence and Change, John D. Millett
HE20 Increasing Basic Skills by Developmental Studies, John E. Roueche
HE21 Marketing Higher Education, David W. Barton, Jr.
HE22 Developing and Evaluating Administrative Leadership, Charles F. Fisher
HE23 Admitting and Assisting Students After Bakke, Alexander W. Astin, Bruce Fuller, Kenneth C. Green
HE24 Institutional Renewal Through the Improvement of Teaching, Jerry G. Gaff
HE25 Assuring Access for the Handicapped, Martha Ross Redden
HE26 Assessing Financial Health, Carol Frances, Sharon L. Coldren
HE27 Building Bridges to the Public, Louis T. Benezet, Frances W. Magnusson
HE28 Preparing for the New Decade, Larry W. Jones, Franz A. Nowotny
HE29 Educating Learners of All Ages, Elinor Greenberg, Kathleen M. O'Donnell, William Bergquist
HE30 Managing Facilities More Effectively, Harvey H. Kaiser
HE31 Rethinking College Responsibilities for Values, Mary Louise McBee
HE32 Resolving Conflict in Higher Education, Jane E. McCarthy
HE33 Professional Ethics in University Administration, Ronald H. Stein, M. Carlota Baca
HE34 New Approaches to Energy Conservation, Sidney G. Tickton
HE35 Management Science Applications to Academic Administration, James A. Wilson
HE36 Academic Leaders as Managers, Robert H. Atwell, Madeleine F. Green
HE37 Designing Academic Program Reviews, Richard F. Wilson
HE38 Successful Responses to Financial Difficulties, Carol Frances
HE39 Priorities for Academic Libraries, Thomas J. Galvin, Beverly P. Lynch
HE40 Meeting Student Aid Needs in a Period of Retrenchment, Martin Kramer
HE41 Issues in Faculty Personnel Policies, Jon W. Fuller
HE42 Management Techniques for Small and Specialized Institutions, Andrew J. Falender, John C. Merson
HE43 Meeting the New Demand for Standards, Jonathan R. Warren
HE44 The Expanding Role of Telecommunications in Higher Education, Pamela J. Tate, Marilyn Kressel
HE45 Women in Higher Education Administration, Adrian Tinsley, Cynthia Secor, Sheila Kaplan

HE46 *Keeping Graduate Programs Responsive to National Needs,* Michael J. Pelczar, Jr., Lewis C. Solmon
HE47 *Leadership Roles of Chief Academic Officers,* David G. Brown
HE48 *Financial Incentives for Academic Quality,* John Folger
HE49 *Leadership and Institutional Renewal,* Ralph M. Davis
HE50 *Applying Corporate Management Strategies,* Roger J. Flecher
HE51 *Incentive for Faculty Vitality,* Roger G. Baldwin
HE52 *Making the Budget Process Work,* David J. Berg, Gerald M. Skogley
HE53 *Managing College Enrollments,* Don Hossler
HE54 *Institutional Revival: Case Histories,* Douglas W. Steeples

Contents

Editors' Notes 1
Hal Hoverland, Pat McInturff, C. E. Tapie Rohm, Jr.

Part 1. Problem Recognition in Higher Education 7

Chapter 1. Recognizing Problems in State Universities 9
Charles J. Ping
Problem recognition is crucial because policy decisions stem from a critical analysis of internal and external environmental factors.

Chapter 2. Stewardship of Resources for 17
Private Higher Education
Douglas R. Moore
Astute management of resources, both financial and human, is an essential feature of administering the private university.

Chapter 3. Mitigating Chaos: California's 25
Community Colleges in the Post-Proposition 13 Period
Gerald C. Hayward
Many of California's community colleges were ill prepared for the financial crisis created by Proposition 13. An analysis of this critical period illustrates ways to avoid disastrous results.

Chapter 4. The Crisis Prevention Analysis Model 33
Hal Hoverland, Pat McInturff, C. E. Tapie Rohm, Jr.
A simple and easily applied paradigm, the Crisis Prevention Analysis model, can be utilized to identify problems in the university.

Part 2. The Search for Solutions 43

Chapter 5. The University Mission Statement: A Tool for 45
the University Curriculum, Institutional Effectiveness, and Change
Maren M. Mouritsen
The mission statement of the university should reflect its values and serve as a guide for its activities.

Chapter 6. Planning and Resource Allocation Management 53
Jack W. Coleman
An effective planning and budgeting system must be integrated into the decision and control process.

Chapter 7. A System for Constraint Removal 63
Reese Parker
Change strategies can be effected systematically by applying a constraint process.

Chapter 8. The Human Factor for Optimal Solutions 73
Lin Bothwell
Educational institutions need to develop self-reliant employees to achieve organizational excellence.

Part 3. Implementation 81

Chapter 9. The Planning-Budgeting Process: Planning 83
as the Basis for Resource Decisions
Neil S. Bucklew, Daniel J. Smith
The planning and budgeting process must be integrated into the decision making process and include constituent participation.

Chapter 10. Looking to the Future: Implementation 91
of a Five-Year Plan
Phillip L. Beukema
To be successful, a comprehensive action plan must have full participation by all constituencies.

Chapter 11. The Professional School Concept: 99
Breaking New Ground
Henry R. Anderson
Creating a new professional school is a difficult process, but it can better serve the profession and enhance the university's prestige.

Chapter 12. Implementing Information Management Strategies 109
C. E. Tapie Rohm, Jr., Pat McInturff, Hal Hoverland
Chief academic managers need to learn about information management strategies to develop the competitive edge.

Conclusion: Putting the Pieces Together 115

Index 117

Editors' Notes

The American university, whether public or private, creates a unique managerial environment. It is hard to imagine another institutional framework where such variety of goals and constraints for both the near and the long term exist simultaneously; further, the proverbial search for truth requires the protection of faculty, while the university's very survival requires the courting of the community by the administrators. Clearly, the tension of the push and pull of the internal political conflicts and struggles is exceeded only by the forces of the external environment.

The forces unleashed during the 1970s focused attention on the external relationships very poignantly. Not only was there the problem of declining enrollments, there were also recessions, oil embargoes, and tax-limitation initiatives, as well as a changing of the guard at the White House. In retrospect, the 1970s marked a period of crisis for higher education; in fact, several schools declared bankruptcy and ceased operation. The decisions that were made ranged from reducing maintenance to terminating tenured senior professors and, as has been stated, closing the doors. As we look back over the last decade or so, one conclusion seems inescapable. It was a period of chaos. But, hopefully, out of the chaos may come more understanding about the operation of institutions of higher education and—more specifically, which is the point of this volume—how academic decision makers were able to effectively navigate the troubled currents of the 1970s and early 1980s. Before we turn to the experiences and candid insights of those who did make the transition, it is first essential to preview the course of this endeavor.

The Academic Enterprise

Probably the easiest way to analyze an institution of higher education is to view it as an amalgamation of ironies. These ironies exist in the domain of its internal operation and create inherent tensions, which are reinforced by its relation to the external environment. And, as will be seen, these inherent tensions that arise within the internal and external environments create a complicated decision matrix for the management of colleges and universities.

The inherent tensions stem in part from the multiplicity of goals and directions that underscore the academic institution. For example, the product of education, the student, is generally an unknown quantity for a substantial number of years. In fact, the professors and administrators may be long gone by the time students realize their potential. Alternatively, the process of research and professional growth is often slow and laborious, while the budgetary process is an annual affair with quarterly reviews. While the goal of the professor is to achieve status and position in the protected halls of academe, administrators move freely from institution to institution. Another group of ironies concerns the students, who more often than not want skills for a job upon leaving the hallowed halls, whereas the liberal arts tradition is concerned with developing a quality future citizenry. This panorama of the operational environment in higher education tends to create inherent tensions that are in turn exacerbated by external stimuli.

The External Environment

The internal paradoxes and institutional ironies were but a fraction of the problems facing institutions of higher learning during the 1970s. The political and economic environment was a cauldron of turbulence, with the fuel crisis of 1972 and the tax-limitation initiatives being the most obvious factors. Adding the political and economic factors to an already internally stressed educational institution is a stimulus for chaos, and chaotic it was.

The oil embargo and fuel crisis of the early 1970s was a devastating blow to the American economy. With the geometric increase of fuel prices, the relationships that served as the bond of the entrepreneurial system were shattered. The result was chaos, bankruptcies, and eventually a severe recession. Although the impact on education was indirect, it was nevertheless crippling. The loss of business activity eroded the tax base, and thus state and federal revenues, which in turn put great pressure on legislatures to engage in a new and relatively unknown process labeled "cutback" budgeting, in which higher education became easy prey for the cutters.

Another external environmental factor of great impact on higher education stemmed from the political arena and the populist tax-initiative revolt of the late 1970s, of which California's Proposition 13 was one of the most famous. Although the initiatives took many forms, the general thrust was to limit governmental spending by limiting tax revenues. In the California example, property tax limitations were instituted by imposing a ceiling and requiring a two-thirds vote to alter taxes or impose new ones.

The impact of these initiatives was manifold. The most obvious impact is that the initiatives simply reduced the funds available to government and led to budget reductions for most govermental units. Further, the initiatives limited future growth, altering long-term projections and budgets. But even in jurisdictions where limitations were not passed, the populist message was clear. Political aspirants jumped on the bandwagon, and even the public colleges and universities were forced to fight for their very survival.

The internal tensions that are inherent in institutions of higher education tend to make decision making a much more nebulous and human interactive process than exists in most bureaucracies. However, given the additional external problems of cutback budgeting and a recession that arose in the 1970s, decision making in academe took on an even more critical character, so that survival and keeping the doors open became the norm. In fact, it was academic management in a time of chaos.

The Decision Matrix

The art of discrimination, or the more socially appealing term *making choices*, is the product of a process generally labeled *decision making*. The history of modern management has focused for the most part on various facets of decision making. Even for those of us intimately involved with management and decision theory, it seems at times that no matter how much science we put into the process, flipping coins may work just as well. The reality, though, is that as the environment tends toward stability and goals become clear, as well as the technology to achieve them, decision making can be very rational. In fact, much of management is directly concerned with the ordering and integration of internal and external environmental variables so as to develop a rational, predictable approach to fashioning choices.

The more difficult approach, and the one of immediate concern, involves the choices that those in power make during a period of chaos. It is during such a period that the science of decision making quickly dissipates into the cloudy areas of gut reactions and whatever-it-takes approaches, when equations do not work because information is not available. These times of uncertainty compound the dilemmas attached to simple problems, and difficult conflicts become exasperating nightmares.

The Mission of Higher Education

From a managerial standpoint, the mission of higher education, as we know, is generally long-term, amorphous, and not easily quantifiable. The importance of a clearly defined mission is, at a minimum, twofold. First, a clearly defined mission provides the organizational touchstone for defining the operational inputs and their ordering. Second, the statement of a mission provides the standard by which to gauge both individual and group efforts. Thus, an organization with a clear mission can calculate organizational efficiency, specifically the number of outputs for a given set of inputs. The obvious difficulty is that the mission of higher education is not clear or well defined, because of the tradition of liberal arts education and an extremely heterogenous constituency.

The liberal arts tradition has been cast in several roles, but primarily we view it as an experiential and socializing process. Neither of these ends lends itself well to short-term specification and evaluation. It is the ongoing proposition, the ideal, that is neither factual nor replicable.

In essence, the elitist notions of the liberal arts tradition attempt to reinforce humanitarian principles and the generation of an enlightened, culturally adept citizenry. The goal may be nice, but how does one measure it? Alternatively, how does one relate the educational process to the achievement of those norms and ideals? One cannot. The socialization function is also amorphous. This is not to say that the process of higher education should shy away from the goals of the liberal arts tradition or even from ideological socialization for a democratic society. Rather, once those directions become a guiding standard, the rational decision process, based on efficiency criteria, becomes difficult to define and even more difficult to implement.

The Constituency

Given the broad goals of education, there is an implicit recognition of a large constituency. The perennial problem that confronts academic managers is that the larger the constituency, the more cross-cutting or competing are the preferences and goals of the groups. Where there is increased heterogeneity, there is a corollary increase in possible conflicts; hence, the need for more compromises. The implication for institutions of higher learning is that they must simultaneously develop focuses that are both less specific and have increased breadth.

The Economic Environment

In a world with infinite resouces, choices would be much less difficult. Since we do live in a world of finite resources, more education requires giving up something else. The reality of academic management is to survive the yearly budgetary cycle. As we have already discussed, the budgets during the 1970s and early 1980s can be best described as lean. It would appear that we have not seen the end of fiscal conservatism at the state and federal levels.

There are several facets of the budgetary process that need to be delineated for us to understand the problems of decision making in higher education during periods of chaos. First, budgets are generally a set of compromises; hence, when substantial intrusions are made into the process, there tends to be an amplification of chaos. Higher education has been caught in a squeeze. With broad goals and a large, heterogeneous clientele, it cannot easily quantify or justify its budgetary position, while its very survival requires it to do so. Moreover, as it identifies various market segments, higher education then becomes directly drawn into the push-pull of the political process. The point clearly is that the academic manager must carefully balance demands of constituents, students, legislators, and faculty in both the short and the long run. One final point that must be understood is that as long as there is pressure to trim budgets, the balancing of interests becomes so precipitous as to be nearly impossible.

When the political environment is in a period of substantial transition, the setting of goals becomes paramount. The emphasis on goals is necessary simply because that is the requisite first step, as well as the standard measure for a rationally based, efficiency-oriented decision process, which is generally what will be found when institutions are competing for limited funds. More simply, the reason that education may or may not get funds is generally going to depend on the product. Recent modern higher education has been labeled as a growth industry providing education to the tidal wave of Baby-Boomers.

The years of growth fostered an attitude of independence and a lack of cost controls and accountability. Cutback budgeting made higher education an easy mark at the state and federal levels. Hence, higher education was on the defensive for the first time since the inception of the growth decades. Thus, decision making at institutions of higher education was an obstacle course by the 1980s. That so many institutions did survive and eventually even began to prosper seems to suggest a real need to understand how decision makers developed and implemented survival strategies.

Decision Making in Academe

To some extent, the direction of this preface has been to reinforce the view that decision making in higher education during the late 1970s and 1980s was devoid of rationalist models. However, this does not mean that decision making was irrational, but only that uncertainty and the breakdown of linkages and predictions meant that there was insufficient information for decision makers to use the quantitative models that were emerging.

The decision process appears to have a consistent and rational form, beginning with problem diagnosis and followed by solutions and strategies and their implementation. Although this is an abbreviated model of the decision process, it seems evident that decision trees, matrices, and frameworks merely break this process down into further subunits, with various emphases placed on these components. The use of these three broad stages provides a clear means of organizing the decisions of administrators during the period of chaos in higher education. Therefore, we have grouped the chapters in this volume into major segments based on problem identification (Part 1), solutions (Part 2), and implementation (Part 3).

Hal Hoverland
Pat McInturff
C. E. Tapie Rohm, Jr.
Editors

Hal Hoverland is dean of the School of Business and Public Administration at California State University, San Bernardino.

Pat McInturff is professor of management in the School of Business and Public Administration at California State University, San Bernardino.

C. E. Tapie Rohm, Jr., is professor of information management and management in the School of Business and Public Administration at California State University, San Bernardino.

Part 1.
Problem Recognition in Higher Education

In retrospect, the impending chaos in higher education should have been evident, but retrospective analysis is a luxury that academic administrators must usually forgo. The push-pull of an ongoing crisis and the continual battle of the budget generally leave decision makers with no time to ponder the "what ifs" of their administrations. Nevertheless, the identification of a disequilibrium or a prospective dysfunction in the institutional environment can lead to solutions and their implementation and thus prevent crisis management. The adage "an ounce of prevention is worth a pound of cure" clearly is appropriate to managers in the academic environment.

Problem identification is one of the most important stages in the decision making process, yet the question that confronts administrators is, first, detection of the problem and, second, ranking the problem in terms of priority with other problems. In the following chapters, three university presidents who confronted the challenge of chaos address the issue of problem identification.

In addition to the candid appraisals of problem recognition that these distinguished individuals present, they also represent different spheres of higher education, since they come from diverse settings, including the public university, the private university, and the community colleges.

The final chapter of Part 1 presents a problem identification framework that can be easily and economically integrated into the university's decision process. Clearly, this framework is not a panacea; rather, it is a synthesis of many of the insights and indicators that the other commentators present. It provides a model for showing the academic manager that there is disequilibrium in the organization and for beginning the process of defining and implementing viable solutions.

Recognizing problems in state universities involves a critical analysis of both internal and external environments and the need to translate this analysis into policy decisions.

Recognizing Problems in State Universities

Charles J. Ping

The challenge is not to recognize problems but to recognize them in a timely fashion and with a will to address the issues they represent. What are the early warning signs? What analyses or quick ratios serve to give early warning of change and the possibility of future institutional crisis? Again, the challenge is not to recognize the problems but to reduce the complex factors to a focus that helps people understand and marshal the forces necessary to address problems. The process generally begins with the use of factual data, but as the implications are grasped, the processes of problem identification on campus quickly become policy analysis and, ultimately, the effort to address the campus climate. In all institutions, the process necessarily moves beyond the campus to determine the interaction of the external and internal environments.

These factors operate in all types of institutions—public and private, comprehensive universities and community colleges. While there are differences, the differences are more matters of degree than of kind. The public university, however, is subject to external policy determination in very direct ways. Even when protected by constitutional or statutory provisions of independence, public universities cannot claim the same degree of freedom that is the birthright of private institutions. The matter was simply stated by the chairman of an appropriations committee in one midwestern state: "The university may have constitutionally mandated autonomy from the political processes," he thundered, "but you cannot eat autonomy!" Further, the immediate environment of public attitudes toward education, the public acceptance of tax levels necessary to support education, the economic condition of the state that provides tax revenue, and political issues stirring the state all have a direct and forceful impact on public institutions. Therefore, the effort to recognize or anticipate problems in state universities requires a concentrated effort to assess this external environment and its interaction with the campus.

A historically low-tax state will most often provide a correspondingly low level of state support for education and other services. This matched set of conditions is unlikely to change dramatically from one year to the next. A high-percentage increase from one budget period to another, while important, is significant primarily in terms of the base from which it starts. Low state support generally also translates into a high dependence on tuition and other sources of income. Yet another illustration of direct dependence on the immediate environment of a particular state is the impact of fluctuations in tax income in states highly dependent on manufacturing industries, particularly industries subject to foreign competition, such as the steel, auto, and glass industries, or in states dependent on extractive industries, such as the coal and oil industries, which are sensitive to price or demand patterns. In such settings, early identification of potential problems is first and foremost a task of scanning the external conditions of the state economy. Useful recognition is a process of anticipating fluctuations in state income, rather than institutional operations or program interests. The sense of public priorities for state appropriations in the minds of legislators, or in the mind of the general public, becomes a critical factor in this analysis. Accordingly, it may frequently be more important in processes of recognition to identify strategies for planned response to problems largely outside the control of the institution.

The place to start in recognizing or, more importantly, anticipating problems is with data analysis. Next comes a set of issues—frequently policy judgments about size and scope of programs, campus aspirations, and the campus climate. With this second-stage analysis, the conscious scanning of the external environment in relation to the internal campus environment takes on a new urgency.

Analysis

The critical ratios for measuring the present health and future prospects of the public university include the analysis of enrollment, staffing, space, and budgets. The use of such ratios clusters around several questions: What changes are occurring over three-, five-, or ten-year intervals? Can usable comparisons be made with other universities? Or, more simply, what is happening over time? Compared to what?

Public universities draw the great majority of their students from within their own states. Figures on demographic trends, high school graduation rates, and general participation levels in higher education are readily available to institutional research offices. The early warning of institutional enrollment problems is a change over time in the number of applications or a relative change in relation to other institutions. Sometimes the change can be a product of state policy, such as a legislative decision that students should bear a larger share of the cost of education or a strict tax-equalization provision leading to sharp increases in out-of-state surcharges and a drop in out-of-state enrollment. A more common causal factor is the creation and the maturing of new, competing state educational institutions, other universities, and community colleges. Often the root of the change lies in general attitudes and perceptions of students, parents, and high school counselors with respect to a particular institution. When the basic data suggest unfavorable comparison with other institutions, then the factual analysis takes a different focus. This effort to determine attitudes and perceptions requires well-designed opinion research for problem recognition.

A second part of the enrollment-ratio analysis is the yield rate for applications. If there is a rapid change in a short period of time, it probably reflects a sharp lowering of the relative position of the institution in terms of ranking of colleges in the minds of students. In contrast, it may reflect a change in the economy of the state, which affects residential and commuter campuses differently. Most of the heavily industrialized states saw this phenomenon in the last recession. Yield rates from applications may also reflect changes other institutions are making in scholarship programs or admissions activity. When this is understood, the analysis then leads to questions of the competitive strategy of the particular institution.

Until recently, a neglected part of enrollment analysis has been the examination of retention and degree-persistence patterns. How many freshmen become sophomores, and sophomores juniors, and so on? What percentage of students persists to completion of degrees? The value of the analysis of trends over time and comparisons with other institutions is the ability to isolate possible causal factors early enough to do something about the problems. Why do students leave? Are there factors that seem to predict attrition? Which of those factors can be addressed by the institution? And, most important, what are the factors that seem to contribute to retention? What can be done to maximize those conditions that contribute to degree persistence?

Enrollment is critical in most public institutions because state funding generally is enrollment-based. If not immediately tied to full-time equivalent (FTE) students, funding is incrementally adjusted over time to reflect growth or decline in numbers enrolled in various programs. A second and largely ignored fact is that many public university budgets are far more tuition-dependent today than ten or twenty years ago. Accordingly, income from state sources as well as from tuition is enrollment-driven. A sharp downward enrollment trend quickly produces budget crises.

The conventional wisdom is that universities are labor-intensive and have little potential to increase the productive ratios of staff either to students taught or to research conducted. There is enough basis in fact in this notion to support the conclusion that the critical ratios are student-to-faculty. Accurate data on changes over time, and comparisons with other institutions of staffing ratio of students/faculty/administrators/support staff, are essential elements to monitor. If these ratios change quickly with rapid decline in student enrollment or with inadequately controlled growth in staffing, then a budget crisis is imminent. This analysis can be expanded in its usefulness by developing data describing limitations in the flexibility of response to enrollment change. The ratio of tenured to nontenured staff is the most obvious example. Other ratios are also important—for example, data that describe increased costs without necessarily increasing income, such as the ratio of full-time faculty to students, or the longevity and the rank distribution of the faculty. To move in the opposite direction, the cost-effective use of part-time faculty or graduate teaching assistants may reflect the quality of education and, therefore, the attractiveness of a particular campus, and may well have a negative impact on enrollment in a competitive environment with a shrinking pool of high school graduates. Monitoring the ratios carefully, comparing how changes occur along a time line, and making comparisons with other institutions become central to the task of anticipating and defining problems.

Plant is often an ignored part of the equations of anticipating problems. Space is expensive. The dollar implications for operating budgets—utility costs, housekeeping, maintenance, periodic remodeling, and major capital investments every twenty-five to thirty years—multiply by many times the original construction investment of campus failities. Thus, ten million dollars in capital construction can represent a potential long-term commitment of a hundred million dollars in operating and remodeling costs over an extended period.

The ratios of space to faculty, space to FTE students, space by type of instructional activity, and the ratio of research space to external funding all provide a major quick analysis for determining trend lines in dollar commitments. A dimension essential to this analysis is the utilization of space. Few campuses have space problems; most have utilization problems. Both station and gross space utilization, over time and in comparison with the patterns at other institutions, can be important early warnings of emerging problems.

Campus construction is too often driven by campus aspirations rather than by program needs. Frequently such efforts to build a campus fail to count the drain of space on available dollars for support of instruction and research activity. Adequate space is important to both instruction and research, but the monitoring of the ratios of space and space utilization is critical to the early definition of potential and actual problems.

People, plant, and budgets provide obvious quick ratios for higher education analysis. Trend lines in budget analysis focus on source and use of funds. The source of funds involves such data as state funds in relation to total budgets, tuition as a percent of total budgets, external funding for research, and private support as a percent of total budget. Again, what is essential is the understanding of what is happening over time and how a given university varies from patterns at similar institutions. While none of the ratios can provide firm conclusions, they can provide important indicators.

Actual changes occurring in institutional life, as opposed to campus rhetoric, are describable by changes at spaced intervals of time in the percentage of total budget dedicated to instructional and departmental budgets. This is to be compared, for example, with the percent of budget being consumed by the important but essentially support activity of physical plant, campus services, and auxiliaries. Changes in research support and overhead recovery, changes in the dollars dedicated to student services, and changes in the library's percent of the budget, all translated into descriptions of changes over time and into comparisons with other institutions, can provide important analyses of the use of funds. Many of the factors influencing these ratios are not institutionally based. They may reflect a rise in energy costs or changes in federal funding for research. If so, then the question of institutional data comparisons becomes increasingly important in answering the question "What can be done to avoid change turning into budget crisis?"

Frequently, actual changes fly in the face of policy pronouncements and goals described in institutional planning. If the language of campus documents fails to have measurable consequences for budget ratios, then whatever the described intent, effective institutional decisions are described by these facts of budget ratios and changes in percent of total over time.

Environment

Factual analysis points to policy issues, but the effort to recognize problems in policy terms involves an exercise in translation. As is true of all translation, finding the right way to convey meaning is a difficult and elusive goal. By far the most troubling aspect of recognizing problems on campus in a timely and effective manner is the obstacle to understanding and acceptance of problems when there are strong disagreements and conflicting interests.

The facts of a sharp drop in enrollment, a budget crisis, and the possibility of reduction in state support are all unmistakable in content and consequences. It requires little insight to recognize these factors as problems. At the same time, the campus environment and the nature of response to the problem may effectively block recognition of the additional problems hidden in these obvious factors. As the expansive decade of the 1960s produced its own tasks (primarily administrative, in the form of the management of opportunities), so, too, the turmoil on campus and declining enrollment and support in the next decades produced management tasks reflecting the crises of the 1970s and 1980s. The urgent has to be dealt with; no administrator would deny this imperative. But when problems reach this dimension, the climate of the campus and the style of crisis management may limit the capacity or will to recognize the underlying issues.

The problems may be defined more by the response to the facts than by the analysis of enrollments or budgets. The closing in to defend against threats of diminished resources, reduction in positions, program discontinuance, separation of campuses into competing fragments, anxiety contributing to loss of the sense of institutional history and future—these are the urgent problems of decline and crisis. Recognizing the problems in the midst of a stress-filled set of proposals to terminate tenured faculty or discontinue colleges and degree programs does not take much sensitivity. The more demanding task is to recognize the problems while they are still in the internal environment.

The scramble to protect and preserve—a defensive posture based on the assumption that whatever exists must at all costs be maintained and is preferable to all imaginable alternatives—manifests the nature of the problem on campuses. Universities historically have been slow to recognize problems and to change. Rudolph (1962) documents that as a consequence of the inability to respond, colleges and universities have been more changed than changing. The recurring problem is defense of the status quo, as opposed to a constant effort to understand the political, social, and economic expectations that give different forms at different times to the missions of universities. Access, for example, has been a dominant expectation for thirty years of rapid expansion in public higher education, but the last decade brought to the fore a new and urgent policy concern with national and individual economic well-being, a growing concern with the American capacity to compete economically in a rapidly changing world economy. This expectation gives form and direction to university research and teaching. It is defined by such varied factors as funding initiatives to support research activity and public policy decisions to create programs of partnership between business and the universities. It is reflected in student selection of courses and major fields. The change is from an emphasis on access to a growing imperative for practical outcome and for quality and excellence. Recognizing the need to reach the expectations of the times and to respond, to consciously shape university life in relation to changing expectations, is itself recognition of a very basic policy issue. The universities are dependent rather than independent institutions. They are dependent on public acceptance, interest, and support.

Another dimension of the response problem is the fragmentation of the university into competing and even warring units. A university typically is a grouping of colleges with related academic departments. These separate units have their own special expertise and interests and, in the university setting, they function as largely independent fiefdoms. Many elements of instruction and research support the wisdom of this specialization—for example, the use of expert judgments on professional competency of staff, requirements of programs, admission of students, and support of research. What has justification in tradition and has demonstrated its worth can at the same time be a very basic problem. This organizational characteristic of universities shapes the response of the institution as a whole to decline in enrollment or budgets. To recognize the lack of a university perspective in the jumble of competing interests is to isolate a problem so pervasive and so debilitating and so very important that it becomes central to effective efforts to address problems. The absence of this understanding cripples most of the efforts to address urgent aspects of the problems. When a university is little more than a collection of separate parts, when the units define their own interests and missions, rather than the university as a whole determining them, and when interests and interdependence of the separate parts are ignored, then chaos is a predictable outcome of crisis. To recognize this fragmentation, in general terms, is to describe the modern university. Beyond this, patterns of decision making, and even structures for decision making that offer no opportunity for discussion and determination beyond the existing units, result in a clustering of parts around a void. The result is decision making by the political processes of compromise among competing interests. When this is the dominant mode of decision making on campus, then there are very basic hindrances to early and effective recognition of problems. Efforts to address the problems involve the creation of new recommending or decision making bodies charged with the task of looking to the future of the institution as a whole.

A third and final characteristic of the internal environment—which, when recognized, can contribute to the identification of the problems lying behind and limiting the effort to respond to budget crises or enrollment decline—is campus mood. Without a strong sense that thought and effort will make a difference in the life of the institution—in short, without the force of hope—problems become overwhelming. The issue then becomes not the monitoring of crisis but the mindset of despair.

Closing in on the future goes hand in hand with a preoccupation to defend what exists. It is the product of the fragmentation of the university into pockets of self-interest, and its root cause is a loss of the essential dynamics of institutional confidence and hope.

The absence of a generally accepted institutional saga, with a sense of institutional history, distinctiveness, contributions, and a vision of a role moving from the past to the present and on to the future, is a very fundamental sign of a problem. Unwillingness to see what is valuable in that history, the tendency to downgrade the present condition of the institution, and loss of the sense of the historic staying power of the university as an institution are all symptomatic. The problem is a loss of basic force and of the essential dynamics of action in effective problem recognition. Such recognition requires a sense that effort can make a difference and that the future can be shaped by thought and action. The nurturing of this conviction is the basic task of institutional leadership.

Reference

Rudolph, F. *The American College.* New York: Knopf, 1962.

Charles J. Ping is president of Ohio University.

The stewardship of financial resources is the key issue facing private universities, but an understanding of human resources, including university personnel, trustees, and alumni, is critical.

Stewardship of Resources for Private Higher Education

Douglas R. Moore

Some issues are common to all of higher education, public and private: the shrinking pool of high school graduates each spring, the eroding position of education within the nation's priorities, decreasing federal financial aid for students, continuing inflation of costs, and growing shortages of qualified faculty as a result of fewer Ph.D. degrees awarded each year. Obviously, there are other issues peculiar to the independent/private colleges and universities. It is equally obvious that there are issues specific to the small private college and to the large private university. This chapter seeks to address some selected issues confronting private/independent institutions of higher education in general, with particular relevance to the small college or university.

The easiest and most popular response to major issues confronting any institution tends to focus on money, both as a problem and as a solution. Lack of funding is perceived as the problem, and larger revenues are seen as providing the solutions. Such a simplistic approach avoids the more fundamental issues and frequently postpones a solution—if not, in fact, rendering it impossible—because of lost opportunity. There are few instances when, in a time of severe crisis, a large and sudden infusion of money has been made available to a college, thereby rescuing it from further deterioration or even death. Few colleges have heard such statements as "You appear to be in dire financial straits, so let me help you!" Such is the substance of fantasy and self-delusion.

Fiscal Responsibility

The private college must address its financial needs first of all as an issue of allocating existing resources and not as an issue of increasing revenues. The stewardship and the husbanding of current resources is the first fiscal commitment it must make. The budget of a college is its manifest plan, representing the priorities and the purposes of the institution. Understanding how, where, and upon whom the college spends its money is the beginning of both wisdom and solvency. Analysis of the budget or spending plan of the college invariably reveals facts about the private college or university: its dependence on tuition revenues, and the cost of personnel as its largest single budget category. In order to live within its means, the college must make choices among programs, activities, and projects.

Tuition dependence is a problem compounded by national demographics, ever-escalating costs for operation, and relative decreases in resources for student aid. Declining enrollments mean declining revenues, the beginning of a spiral downward, as fewer resources render the college less attractive and in turn cause enrollments to decline even further. Student financial aid is absolutely critical for the private college to compete with the public institution. Otherwise, the private college can admit only those who can pay full tuition and must devolve to a college solely for the affluent.

Since World War II, federal and state financial aid have helped provide students with a choice between the public and private sectors of higher education. Such aid has suffered a relative decline in the last ten years or so, and there is every indication that this circumstance is likely to get worse. Before the infusion of federal and state money for student aid, scholarships and loan funds were probably the most popular needs addressed by private philanthropy. Colleges and universities have de-emphasized such needs over the past thirty years, and contributors have channeled their gifts into other areas. It is imperative that private colleges re-establish student aid as a priority in fundraising activities.

A number of colleges, including the University of Redlands, have established student loan programs in recent years. These loan funds have been a response not only to threats of governmental reductions in such funds but also to flaws, if not inequities, in the government programs. At Redlands, the university in effect became the guarantor of student loans. This program immediately became very attractive to students and their families and provided invaluable assistance to students who might not have been able to attend the university. The program also stimulated two large gifts to the university for support of the loan fund.

Reduction in personnel costs is an essential, though painful, series of decisions that must be faced by most colleges. As enrollments grew in the post-World War II period, there was commensurate growth in programs, activities, and personnel. In the current era of declining enrollments, appropriate reductions must be made. These decisions involve the setting of priorities, weighing of programs against institutional purposes, and the trauma of terminating the employment of some people as positions are eliminated. It is a singularly unattractive prospect for an individual to benefit from the termination of a colleague, yet it is precisely through this process that resources are freed, not only to balance budgets but also to reallocate funds. It is a simple fact that salaries can be increased if there are fewer salary lines in the budget. Doing fewer things but doing them better can be an important manifestation of stewardship.

There are at least three further elements essential to the resolution of the fiscal issue: endowment management, care of facilities, and effective fundraising.

Endowment. The endowment of a private university represents its long-term health and security. That endowments must be increased needs neither defense nor elaboration. Management of endowment is both the responsibility and the stewardship of trustees. The management of a small endowment is no less important than the management of a large and complex portfolio of investments. Regardless of the good intentions, high integrity, and even financial knowledge of trustees, it is impossible for a committee of the board to manage an endowment adequately. Trustees are extremely busy people and usually cannot devote the interest, skills, or time necessary to guarantee adequate care of the university's investments. While trustees should set policies reflecting an appropriate balance between growth and earnings and must set performance goals for the endowment, a professional management firm is necessary to maximize the effectiveness of endowment management. Trustees should evaluate those who manage the portfolio, rather than attempt to deal with a volatile economy via quarterly or even monthly meetings devoted to actual management of investments.

Care of Facilities. Private institutions obviously do not have access to state appropriations for capital improvements, whether for new buildings and equipment or for maintenance and refurbishment. Consequently, the private institution frequently defers maintenance, with the result that buildings and equipment deteriorate to the point that maintenance costs begin to rise at an almost exponential rate. Because maintenance is at first a hidden need, budget priorities tend to focus on more obvious demands on resources. By the time facilities show dramatic need of attention, the costs are frequently prohibitive. Adequate and systematic attention to physical plant and equipment must be a manifest priority in institutional budgets.

Recovering from long-deferred maintenance problems is extraordinarily difficult. One avenue open to private universities is the use of tax-exempt bonds. Through the California Educational Facilities Act, independent colleges and universities in California have been able to float bond issues both individually and collectively, thus amortizing facility and equipment improvements over twenty-year periods.

Effective Fundraising. It is obvious to anyone in higher education that tuition can never be high enough to cover the true costs of attending college. For the private institution, the differential must be covered by endowment income, auxiliary enterprises, and raising money. It is not only possible but imperative for every independent college or university to have an effective staff for development and institutional advancement. Regardless of the size of the institution or the restrictions on its annual budget, there is no wiser investment than a productive staff of people committed to fundraising.

Annual budgets can and must be augmented by successful annual funds, which draw on the loyalty and affection of alumni and friends. Capital needs must be met, at least partially, by regular, systematic, and carefully directed capital campaigns. Long-term needs of the institution must be addressed through a program of planned giving. The planned giving program of a private institution may be the most effective and reasonable enterprise for building endowment. Trusts, gift annuities, pooled income funds, and bequests are instruments allowing benefactors to make large contributions accruing to the university in later years, while permitting the donor to receive income in the interval. Pomona College, through its "Pomona Plan," has had for several decades one of the most effective planned, or deferred, giving programs in the nation.

Mission and Purpose

This analysis is but the mechanics or the infrastructure of the university—necessary, but only as a means of achieving the goals of the institution. The biggest and most common mistake of the smaller private institution is in attempting to be all things to all people, imitating the large independent university or the public institution. Knowing what it uniquely is and where it is going is no less important for a university than for an individual. Possessing a clearly articulated, well-considered statement of mission and purpose and implementing it programatically allows the university to identify whom it will serve. In the commercial parlance of the day, this process positions the college with respect to its market. The priorities of the institution, the ambiance of the campus, the kind of faculty it recruits, the supporters it cultivates, and the prospective students it seeks to enroll all derive from the definition of the institution stated in its mission. This axiom is true for Stanford or Harvard, Swarthmore or Carleton, and probably has never been more imperative than right now, given the nation's demographics.

The statement and implementation of mission and purpose defines the university, enables it to plan rather than react, gives it its unique character, and inspires loyalty from its alumni and friends. The mission of the college is its identity, providing a profile of visibility among its intended constituents. Good students choose among institutional styles and character and among defined purposes. Benefactors give money to institutions in which they believe deeply and about which they care greatly.

Resources for Independent Institutions

As already discussed, stewardship of resources is the key issue facing private/independent higher education. However, the discussion thus far has focused on fiscal and physical resource management. The most significant resource available to and underutilized by these colleges and universities is the people associated with them. Cultivation, enlistment, and utilization of people is the paramount priority for every private university. Certainly the faculty, administration, and staff of these institutions have demonstrated loyalty and even sacrificial commitment; for the most part, they are underpaid and often exploited. Leaving aside the significance of this particular resource, however, it is appropriate to address the other human resources. Proper enlistment and use of these others will do a great deal to improve the circumstances of faculty and other university personnel.

Trustees. The governing board of an independent university, in contrast to the public institution, is a self-perpetuating body, freed from political appointments and partisan conflicts. This fact is one of the unique features of independent higher education and offers a latitude and flexibility not always employed to the institution's advantage. Governing boards hire and fire presidents and chancellors, no small responsibility, but aside from this function their major task is identifying, cultivating, and enlisting new trustees. This responsibility may in fact be the area in which governing boards fail most often. More often than not, recruitment of new trustees is handled in a casual and haphazard manner, yet there is no function more important than that of selecting persons appropriate to the governing board.

Every governing board of every independent institution of higher learning should have a standing committee whose singular task is trustee development. The University of Redlands has such a committee, which meets monthly for the sole purpose of developing trustees. This group evaluates sitting trustees, specified criteria for trustee selection (ensuring diversity and broad representation), identifies and studies potential candidates, develops strategies for cultivating candidates, and proposes for election those who are appropriate and ready to join the board. It is only through such a systematic and thorough process that a strong governing board can be developed and maintained. Certainly, the private university must have on its board persons of influence and wealth because the board is the central force in meeting the fiscal needs of the institution. The board also must have members with particular knowledge, skills, and competence, regardless of their degree of wealth or influence. There are few responsibilities more important to a private college than the selection of a trustee, and many people feel there is no greater honor than to be asked to serve on the board of an institution in whose purpose they believe deeply.

Volunteers. Few public colleges enjoy as much affection and loyalty as almost any independent college, large or small, mediocre or prestigious, gains from its alumni and friends, yet this reservoir of commitment and goodwill remains for many only a potential force and is too often untapped. Not only is it rare for alumni financial support to exceed 15 percent of the total alumni, but alumni are also seldom asked to do anything for their college or university. Alumni, parents, and friends of higher education represent the best-educated, most articulate, and most successful people in this society. They are the products of the institution and the best representative it has, yet their knowledge and skills are underutilized.

Obviously, the alumni and friends of the private college must be asked for money. They ought to be asked also for counsel and advice. Most important, they should be enlisted to represent the institution. Give them a job to do, encourage them, recognize them, and watch the results!

Within the last ten years, the University of Redlands has followed the practice of several other independent universities in enlisting alumni and friends for assistance in two important projects: recruitment of students and raising money for the annual fund.

The Redlands Admissions Assistance Program has more than five hundred volunteers throughout the United States. Volunteers are given the names of prospective students whom Redlands wants to attract. These volunteers telephone students, host gatherings, and generally provide information and a personal contact with prospective students. It takes money and staff time in support of this program, but that time and money multiply the personnel available to represent the university effectively.

The University Relations and Development Office began the use of alumni and friends in fundraising several years ago through its Telefund. At strategic points throughout the country, Telefund nights are set up each year, usually in the office complex of a volunteer, where there are several telephone lines. Alumni and friends then telephone other alumni and friends in that area, asking them for a pledge to the annual fund. The money raised is important but, in the long term, the most significant result is the personal contact, the conversation about the university, and often the healing of some wound the university had not even realized existed.

The circumstances facing all of higher education for the rest of this century can only exacerbate the usual, if not chronic, issues facing the private sector. Recognizing these issues, aggressively cultivating both fiscal and personnel resources, and wisely utilizing all these assets ensures a healthy diversity in American higher education. Such diversity is absolutely essential to this society. Our society itself must recognize the value of both the public and the independent university. If private institutions recognize the problems and opportunities confronting them and recognize the resources available for responding, then this society will respond as it always has done, with generosity and commitment, to those things it values most.

Douglas R. Moore has been president of the University of Redlands since 1978, after serving as president of Mankato State University in Minnesota.

The experience of California's community colleges in coping with the crisis created by the passage of Proposition 13 suggests critical elements necessary for recognizing problems and mitigating chaos.

Mitigating Chaos: California's Community Colleges in the Post-Proposition 13 Period

Gerald C. Hayward

As Paul Valéry so succinctly put it, "The problem with our times is that the future isn't what it used to be." There are many of us who would relish the notion of going back to simpler, less chaotic, more predictable futures. That is purely wishful thinking, particularly for those of us who toil in the community college vineyard. The future promises to be more, not less, complex. The major problem will be to recognize that uncertainty will continue to be a fact of life and to develop plans and strategies that can accommodate and shape that reality. Educational leadership, whether it is in administration, among the faculty, or within boards of trustees, will be more difficult. Leaders will have less control over their own destinies, and the role played by external forces affecting their leadership capabilities promises to be even greater. Thus, leaders of the future may well have to major in ambiguity and minor in conflict resolution.

California Community Colleges—The Context

In 1986, California community colleges are just now slowly emerging from the shock and aftershocks of the infamous Jarvis-Gann-sponsored Proposition 13, overwhelmingly approved by the California electorate in

1978. To say the colleges were unprepared to deal with the chaos created by its passage is an understatement. Proposition 13 affected every phase of college operations, and districts found themselves woefully ill equipped to deal with problems of such magnitude. An old Chinese proverb reminds us that "out of the mud grows the lotus." Hopefully, a review of the post-Proposition 13 era in California can be instructive in recognizing and coping with future crises. I have chosen to focus on the California situation—first because I know it, second because it represents a significant portion of the national community college movement, and finally because if holds important clues for actively affecting the unpredictable future. I will concentrate of three general areas: finance, mission, and governance.

Finance

Since the passage of Proposition 13, with its resultant loss of revenue and its revenue shift from local taxpayers to the state, California's community college funding situation can be characterize by two words: inadequate and uncertain. Since that time, funding on a per-student basis has fallen far short of keeping pace with inflation and, even more significant, has been highly unpredictable. There have been six different funding arrangements in the last eight years, often with precipitous changes in community college finance and in the incentives and disincentives that are inherent in any funding mechanism. Inadequacy of funding and changes of the type and magnitude that have occurred during the post-Proposition 13 period have made it extremely difficult for districts to plan for and manage their institutions. This high degree of uncertainty led one wag to comment that in California community colleges, "long-range planning is planning for the next six months and perpetuity is defined as one year." In addition, Proposition 13 removed from local districts the ability to levy local ad valorem property taxes, even with the consent of the district's constituents. For all practical purposes, decisions about the level of per-student funding, as well as about the maxmimum number of students eligible for funding, are now made at the state level, primarily through the state budget mechanism. Local districts have in effect been precluded from the most critical decisions that affect their funding destinies. The irrepressible Howard Jarvis argued for the passage of Proposition 13 by saying it was time to remove decisions from "those popcorn balls" in Sacramento. A cruel irony for Mr. Jarvis and the proponents of Proposition 13 is that "those popcorn balls" now effectively control the major funding decisions for local governments, including community colleges.

Mission

California's community colleges have historically had a diverse and comprehensive mission. In fact, as one looks carefully at the mission of the colleges, one is struck by its remarkable consistency over time. However, the focus of that mission, and the emphasis each college has placed on various aspects, has changed, often to reflect the special needs of the many communities the colleges serve. Community colleges may even have been victimized by their own success at being responsive. The authors of the 1960 California Master Plan Commission saw the community colleges as the major providers of students for transfer to the state colleges and universities, with adjunct vocational education, general education, and community service functions. The colleges' responses to local pressures for community service and to the growing demand for lifelong learning led to rapid growth in those areas of the typical California community college curriculum and to a relative de-emphasis on the transfer function during the 1960s and 1970s. It can be argued that the community college response to local demands outstripped state public policy support for these aspects of the mission. When the legislature and the governor were forced to face the difficult task of reassessing the state's priorities for funding in response to the diminishing resources available after the passage of Proposition 13, community colleges found themselves in a highly vulnerable position. The 1982 legislature, faced with a deficit of unprecedented dimensions, eliminated $30 million from community college budgets and directed the state Board of Governors to discontinue all state support for recreational and avocational courses. Clearly, in times of great fiscal stress, district responsiveness to local needs is not an eminently salable commodity in the state legislature. In sum, while responsiveness has produced an unparalleled diversity among the colleges, a great strength locally, it has simultaneously created a major problem in attempting to describe to public policy makers what the colleges are all about. In the competition for state funds, relative to institutions and agencies that had clearer, better-defined missions. It is abundantly clear that community colleges of the future simply cannot continue to do all the things they have historically done, without a strong public policy commitment to their role and the necessary funds to carry out their mission.

Governance

California's community college governance structure is a direct outgrowth of its historic linkage with secondary schools. It provides the framework for what was originally intended to be a highly decentralized governance system designed to focus on responsiveness to local needs. In fact, the legislature's charge to the Board of Governors contains the following directive: "The work of the board shall at all times be directed to maintaining and continuing, to the maximum degree permissible, local autonomy and control in the administration of the community colleges." This arrangement served the state and the colleges adequately during the period when funding sources were primarily local. However, with the passage of Proposition 13 and the resultant shift of funding authority from the local jurisdictions to the state, California's community colleges became a governance anomaly; in no other state is the linkage between funding and operational control so bifurcated. The recently completed Berman and Weiler study of California community colleges (1985, p. 20) stated the governance dilemma succinctly: "Both local trustees and the State Board of Governors lack key elements of the capacity to govern. As a consequence, key decisions affecting the colleges are often made by the state legislature—that is, in the political arena. This has further weakened local autonomy and has clouded the issue of where leadership resides."

Proposition 13 totally changed the landscape of California's 106 community colleges. It not only reduced resources available at the state and local level but also changed, perhaps irreversibly, the locus of power and the governance dynamic. Abruptly and unexpectedly, the community colleges, historically reliant on the goodwill of their local constituents, were thrust into a new, less familiar arena—the state—and were forced to compete in the annual battle for the state's scarce resources. As revenues diminish, legislatures and governors increasingly scrutinize the expenditure of public funds. This added scrutiny places institutions with multiple purposes and less clear functions at a distinct disadvantge in the competition for resources. In addition, the centralization of the process for appropriation and allocation of funds demands a higher degree of accountability than the historically decentralized community colleges have as yet been able to muster.

It would be inaccurate to attribute to Proposition 13 the responsibility for every community college governance problem. Other significant forces have affected the power and control once exercised by locally elected trustees and community college chief executive officers. At the state level, the authority of the state Board of Governors and the state higher education coordinating agency has increased dramatically, as has the role of the four-year educational institutions. For example, as state resources have become scarcer, and in light of a diminishing pool of high school graduates, the four-year institutions have expanded recruiting efforts, and campuses of the University of California have adopted unilateral policy changes to increase their percentages of lower-division students. This has resulted in a diminished pool of transfer-eligible students for the community colleges. Locally, trustees have seen their autonomy eroded by the advent of collective bargaining, as well as by the loss of their ability to determine revenues effectively. Administrators have watched their authority wane because of the increased activism (some would say administrative interference) of local trustees and increased roles of special-interest groups in the governance process. Of particular note in California has been the growing involvement of faculty in trustee elections. All these external factors have had the cumulative effect of reducing the authority of local administrators.

It is unlikely that these problems will abate in the near future. In times of stress and precipitous change, unless community college administrators alter their strategies of coping with the uncertainties they face, their ability to affect the future of the institutions for which they are held accountable will be marginal.

In order to deal effectively with chaos, the initial task for policy makers is to recognize the context within which policy is made. Community college leaders will face an ambiguous future, armed with a diminished capacity to direct their institutions and, unless they are responsive, their own professional fates as well. Does this mean that there is no hope? Not at all. What it does mean is that community college leaders will have a unique opportunity to learn from the post-Proposition 13 period, to play a critical role in shaping the destinies of their institutions by recognizing the new context, and to take positive steps to affect their futures. What is required is an enhanced ability on the part of the colleges to be able to respond quickly and ably to change. The promise is an increased capacity to mitigate chaos.

Problem Recognition

It would be folly for college leaders to spend a great deal of time conjuring up all the potential problems their institutions may face in the future. The list may well be infinite. What is eminently more sensible and much more manageable is to identify the processes necessary for assessing and dealing with future problems as they arise.

Simply put, the relevant question is not how to recognize problems but whether adequate systems and processes are in place to deal with potential problems. For illustrative purposes, I have chosen to concentrate on three areas—information systems, planning, and decision making—and to pay particular attention to the status of these systems and processes in the era immediately following the passage of Proposition 13.

Information Systems

At the heart of any sound problem recognition/decision making system lies a soundly based information system. The first element of an effective system includes the capability to describe the district's current financial situation and to make solid projections about its future. A recent California review of community college districts that were in severe financial difficulty uncovered the following patterns: inadequate ending balances to withstand revenue shortfalls, deficit spending (expenditures exceeding revenues in any given year), inadequate enrollment projection mechanisms, and staffing patterns that did not allow the district to respond to the financial crisis in the short time frame allowed. At least some of these problems were exacerbated by inadequate information systems. In any labor-intensive enterprise (85 percent of the typical California community college's budget is devoted to employee-related expenditures), it is vital that the college have longitudinal data and adequate analysis about such basic elements as salaries, workload, average age, sex, ethnicity, and credentials for both full- and part-time instructors. Although the vast majority of colleges maintained these data files, I was amazed that some did not. When revenues are restricted, the absence of high-quality, reliable data about the financial characteristics of the district is suicidal.

Another major component is information about the clients of the system, the students. On this dimension, community colleges in California were woefully inadequate. Few colleges, for example, had complete information systems that adequately described the nature of their student bodies. Although most had adequate information regarding weekly student contact hours, most did not routinely require high school transcripts. Few had adequate assessment information about student skills. Very few had any information about student goals, and even fewer were able to ascertain whether students were making progress toward meeting those goals. These times of economic retrenchment call for improved retention efforts, which were crippled by inadequate information about student characteristics.

A process for collecting adequate information about prospective clients was also a rarity. Admittedly, such information is difficult and expensive to obtain, but the planning process and the ability to respond to future needs makes the gathering of such information a necessity. In the early 1980s, several community colleges were unable to respond, because of information system inadequacies, to the fact that the numbers of high school graduates in their attendance areas were declining. That, coupled with declining revenues, created an immense planning problem

A critical but often overlooked source of information is the community. For planning purposes, it is essential to include information about the perceptions of the citizens, both state and local, regarding the mission of the colleges. As we discovered in post-Proposition 13 California, there was confusion and lack of popular consensus about what community colleges were doing and what they ought to be doing. That confusion, of course, affected the perceptions of policy makers and placed community colleges at a serious disadvantage in the competition for state funding. Adequate information about public attitudes simply did not exist immediately following the passage of Proposition 13. Public opinion polling about attitudes toward the colleges is an important but often neglected component of an adequate information system. When revenues were plentiful, as they had been in California prior to Proposition 13, there was little downside risk, and hence little incentive to invest in detailed information systems. If community colleges expect to fare well in achieving adequate funding and to plan well, an improved information system is a must.

Planning

The cruel irony of the planning process is that planning has been seen as less important in times of plentiful resources, but it is virtually impossible in times of crisis, as the institutional constituencies move to protect their own special interests. Being open and explicit about expenditure priorities is infinitely more difficult in times of scarce resources. Comprehensive planning must become an integral part of the district's mode of operation in good times and bad. Unfortunately, California's community colleges, as well as higher education institutions generally, were inadequately prepared for the more complex strategies involved in planning for retrenchment. An ongoing planning process that includes alternatives and contingencies is a major element in determining a district's ability to respond to chaos.

Decision Making

A superior information system and a quality planning process do the district little good if the ability to convert the results of planning into action is lacking. Too little attention has been paid to the politics of converting plans to policy. All too frequently, district administrators found that their recommendations for returning the district to at least a semblance of fiscal stability lacked the political consensus to take effect—that is, to overcome the resistance from special constituencies whose major priority was to protect particular clients or programs. In many such cases, the root cause of the political problem was the lack of attention given to building, within the district, the kinds of political support needed to effect change in any democratic process.

Top-down planning, while not enthusiastically embraced, is often tolerated in times of plenty; it is rarely effective in troubled times. The uncertainties of the future call for a much more inclusive process, based on a collegial concern about the future viability of the institution. It requires participation by all affected parties, trustees, administrators, faculty, staff, students, and the community in the decision making process. It requires an agreed-upon, clearly understood data base. It requires consensually determined, alternative sets of assumptions and fully disclosed information concerning the often arcane budget and financial conditions the district faces. Finally, and most important, it requires a sense that decisions are made openly and that a general climate of fairness exists. Without such an institutional ambience, the district will be unable to respond adequately, if at all, to crisis situations.

Conclusion

Unfortunately, most of California's community colleges were ill-prepared for Proposition 13. The information system, particularly as it related to students, was inadequate; the planning process, particularly as it related to plans for retrenchment, was insufficient; and attention to the decision making process was a rarity. In spite of all this, community colleges somehow managed to survive, and almost all of them are actively taking steps to ensure that the next crisis, when it occurs, will not have such a devastating impact. In the years since Proposition 13, the Board of Governors and the local districts have taken several positive steps to improve local capacity to respond to uncertainty. Giant steps have been taken to improve student information (Field Research Corporation, 1984). Such processes as the Board of Governor's matriculation plan (Chancellor's Office, 1984), aimed at improving student retention and persistence, are rapidly being implemented. Comprehensive planning efforts, once a rarity, are now a matter of course (Board of Governors, 1985; Chancellor's Office, 1985). Much, of course, remains to be done, especially in building a local climate that focuses on the institution's viability and not on special client or program interests. As the state's fiscal situation improves, and as the colleges once again have some breathing room, it is incumbent that the processes be put in place not to mitigate crises when they inevitably occur. The fact that California's community colleges survived Proposition 13 is testimony to their remarkable resilience. The fact that districts are purposefully acting to improve their capacity to mitigate chaos bodes well for their collective future.

References

Berman, Weiler Associates. *A Study of California's Community Colleges.* Vol. 2, *Findings.* Berkeley, Calif.: Berman, Weiler Associates, 1985.
Board of Governors, California Community Colleges. *1985 Basic Agenda.* Sacramento: Chancellor's Office, California Community Colleges, 1985.
Chancellor's Office, California Community Colleges. *Student Matriculation: A Plan for Implementation in the California Community Colleges.* Sacramento: Chancellor's Office, California Community Colleges, 1984.
Chancellor's Office, California Community Colleges. *Contours of Change.* Sacramento: Chancellor's Office, California Community Colleges, 1985.
Field Research Corporation. *A Survey of Community College Enrollment Conducted as Part of Fee Impact Study.* Sacramento: Chancellor's Office, California Community Colleges, 1984.

Gerald C. Hayward served for six years as chancellor of the California Community Colleges. He is currently Distinguished Senior Visiting Lecturer at the University of California, Berkeley, and serves as Sacramento director of project PACE (Policy Analysis for California Education).

Many universities are facing serious financial problems. The Crisis Prevention Analysis model offers a framework to analyze problems simply and quickly.

The Crisis Prevention Analysis Model

Hal Hoverland, Pat McInturff, C. E. Tapie Rohm, Jr.

Modern colleges and universities are facing what may be one of the most important periods in their history. At stake is their very survival. Already, such institutions as Westminster College (Biemiller, 1983), Shaw College at Detroit ("Shaw College. . . ," 1984), and Eisenhower (Biemiller, 1983), have closed their doors or sought protection from creditors under United States bankruptcy laws. Clearly, one does not have to spend much time researching the problems to understand that they are real (Barnett and O'Neill, 1981, "A Roundup on Layoffs. . . ," December 8, 1982). The problems include declining enrollments, changing demographics, uncertain economic conditions, and fluctuations in the political environment. The remedies, too, must be developed and implemented with a seriousness that is predicated on survival. These remedies have become as pervasive as the problems—satellite programs, adjunct faculty, endowment campaigns, and credit for life experience. To reiterate the obvious, academia is in a difficult period.

What may not be so clear is the extent or the depth of the problems and forces confronting educational institutions. The societal cost of closing the doors of educational institutions should be of concern to all citizens.

The most obvious groups affected by cutbacks and shutdowns of colleges and universities are the students, teachers, administrators, and staff, yet there are multiplier effects on the community, which may not always be readily evident. Finally, and less evident, is the impact on the democratic traditions of American life.

Hopefully, the point has been made that these are very distressing times for colleges and universities. Educational institutions forced to close have generally been unable to re-emerge as viable entities. The initial conclusion is that once a collegiate institution is caught in the position of filing for bankruptcy or using other extreme survival strategies, it is probably too late to install a financial planning and control system. Thus, it is imperative that institutions apprise themselves early and quickly of prospective and existing problems.

The importance of developing an analytical framework to identify problems confronting academic managers should be self-evident. Although there are computerized financial planning models—for example, CAMPUS and RRPM (Massey and Hopkins, 1981)—some universities may not have the capability to implement such systems. Furthermore, a simple model has the advantage of swift and easy implementation and can indicate the need for immediate analysis and action. The purpose here is to present a framework that can be used to prevent a major financial crisis or at least generate warning indicators to keep the institution viable. The model that will be described is the Crisis Prevention Analysis (CPA) framework. As the name implies, it is a framework whose operational goal is to anticipate and prevent the need for crisis-oriented management. The model was developed by synthesizing recurring patterns and events associated with institutions that have confronted or are confronting financial crises. Once the phenomena have been defined, a scaling system is utilized and applied to the selected institution. The results then become indicators of financial status, weak areas, or other specific, critical areas.

In one sense, educational institutions share a critical problem with other social organizations: the need for clear, concise information and a framework to integrate that information into the goals and aspirations of the organization. For educational institutions, one goal that has become of continuing concern is simple survival. To achieve that goal, information and a means of generating it to ensure survival may be critical in some circumstances. The CPA model rests on two foundations. First, the historical basis consists of a survey of cases, histories, and conflicts that have been perceived as relevant and important at those institutions whose survivial was in doubt or whose doors did close. The second basis is the development of a management decision-oriented framework that can integrate problem areas into a set of predictive variables so that institutional administrators can be aware of and develop solutions and strategies before problems become critical.

Application of the Crisis Prevention Analysis (CPA) Model

The Crisis Prevention Analysis (CPA) model covers the four major areas of Fiscal, Faculty and Staff, Support Functions, and Goals and Attitudes, with specific items in each area. Suggested evaluation criteria are delineated in Exhibit 1. The CPA Model (Exhibit 2) is a self-appraisal instrument designed for total possible score of 100 points. The ratings of Inadequate, Poor, Satisfactory, and Good are assigned values of 1, 2, 3, and 4, respectively. Since there is a total of twenty-five items in the four categories, the best possible score is 100 points. Each of the four ratings of Inadequate, Poor, Satisfactory, and Good would total 25, 50, 75, and 100 points, respectively, and so these scores can be used as guidelines for an overall rating. In addition, category scores can be analyzed in the same way to evaluate the institution's strengths or weaknesses in each of the categories.

In implementing the CPA model, it is important that more than one administrator independently score the inventory and then make comparisons. An optimal number of scorers would be five, although the number could depend on the size of the institution and the positions of the particular administrators. Using more than one administrator should reduce the bias of the appraisal and also highlight administrators' differing perceptions. Having a number of administrators independently score the CPA inventory is a process similar to the Delphi method, in which consensus is used to determine the best alternative.

The CPA model may also be utilized by subunits within an institution, for example, colleges, schools, departments, but these applications would depend on the size of the institution and the autonomy of the units.

The CPA model should be generally adaptable to most educational institutions, regardless of size, location, and orientation, but the unique characteristics of an institution may be considered when applying the model. For example, an institution may be public or private, have a student body that is primarily local or from all parts of the country, have a research or teaching orientation, and have a resident or commuter student population. In reviewing the unique characteristics of the institution, an administrator may want to assign different weights to the various items on the CPA inventory. However, the authors feel that the process of self-evaluation is of primary importance; therefore, the model should be applied initially in its original form. In applying the model, administrators are sensitized to the various aspects of the institution's operations and are then in a better position to make changes in the model, although adapting the model to account for unique characteristics may reflect the bias of the administrators and color the self-appraisal.

The CPA model has some important features. It is simple, easy to

Exhibit 1. Crisis Prevention Analysis Evaluation Criteria

A. *Fiscal*
1. Enrollment — Enrollment changes, potential college populations
2. Tuition — Tuition changes, financial aid, tuition as percent of discretionary income
3. Endowment — Endowment changes, income from endowment as percent of operating income
4. Continuing education — Income changes, numbers of courses and students
5. Alumni — Percent of alumni in alumni organization, quantity and quality of alumni projects
6. Capital budget — Expenditure changes (total and in high-technology and high student demand areas)
7. Maintenance — Budget change, percent of total budget, long-term maintenance plan

B. *Faculty and Staff*
1. Benefits — Changes in benefit package and instructional support
2. Salaries — Salary changes, comparability with other educational institutions
3. Personnel turnover — Percent of total personnel (by faculty and staff and by department)
4. Collective bargaining — Potential for unionization or effects of collective bargaining
5. Temporary faculty — Percent of total faculty (by university and by discipline)
6. Student-faculty ratios — By discipline and level (lower division, upper division, graduates)
7. Attitudes — Interviews, faculty senate discussions

C. *Support Functions*
1. Library — Changes in holdings and hours of operation
2. Placement — Employer contacts, number of employers interviewing, number of graduates placed
3. Business office — Rate of return on investments, cost control and reporting, purchasing analysis
4. Development office — Number and amount of grants and contributions, interpersonal relations between development office and other campus units
5. Community relations — Personnel participation in community organization and projects
6. Marketing — Enrollment changes and patterns, marketing activity analysis
7. Student life — Quantity and quality of events and activities, student participation, surveys

D. *Goals and Attitudes*
1. Strategic planning — How comprehensive, how developed, how implemented
2. Innovation — Climate for innovation, rate of implementation of new ideas
3. Image appraisal — Surveys, interaction with external groups and individuals
4. Institutional attitude — Faculty senate discussions, appraisals by department chairs and staff

Exhibit 2. Crisis Prevention Analysis Model

		(1) Inadequate	(2) Poor	(3) Satisfactory	(4) Good	Total
A.	**Fiscal**					
	1. Enrollment					
	2. Tuition					
	3. Endowment					
	4. Continuing Education					
	5. Alumni					
	6. Capital Budget					
	7. Maintenance					
	Category Totals					
B.	**Faculty & Staff**					
	1. Benefits					
	2. Salaries					
	3. Personnel Turnover					
	4. Collective Bargaining					
	5. Temporary Faculty					
	6. Student-Faculty Ratios					
	7. Attitudes					
	Category Totals					
C.	**Support Functions**					
	1. Library					
	2. Placement					
	3. Business Office					
	4. Development Office					
	5. Community Relations					
	6. Marketing					
	7. Student Life					
	Category Totals					
D.	**Goals & Attitudes**					
	1. Strategic Planning					
	2. Innovation					
	3. Image Appraisal					
	4. Institutional Attitude					
	Category Totals					
TOTALS						

implement, and has a readily understandable scoring system. It forces administrators to go through the process of critically looking at various aspects of the institution's operations. It also has been designed independently of the institution and therefore minimizes the infusion of self-fulfilling prophecy. Naturally, the worth of any self-appraisal technique depends on both the judgment process and the actions taken after self-appraisal. In the judgment process, the ratings should be made as objectively as possible and, as previously mentioned, should be done by more than one administrator. After the self-appraisal, some definite decisions should be made and implemented. The changes may be major or minor, but the Crisis Prevention Analysis process is predicated on the fundamental assumption that it is easier to take action prior to a major crisis. An institution has much more flexibility and more options for correcting deficiencies while it is still a viable entity than when it is in serious financial difficulty. The number of educational institutions that have had to close their doors in recent years attests to the seriousness of this problem.

Although the Crisis Prevention Analysis model is not a panacea, it is a useful analytical tool for educational administrators. The process of internal analysis is extremely important, and the CPA model provides an analytical framework to review the spectrum of the institution's activities. The results of applying the CPA model can then be used as an agenda for action to improve the institution's operations.

Concepts Underlying the CPA Model

The Crisis Prevention Analysis model focuses on four primary areas of academic management: Fiscal, Faculty and Staff, Support Functions, and Goals and Attitudes. Although these are arbitrary categories and are bound to involve some overlapping, they were developed to provide a focus and structure for academic managers to analyze their institutions' strengths and weaknesses quickly and easily.

Fiscal. Primary revenue sources for universities are state and federal funds, tuition, private gifts, grants, and continuing education programs. The relative proportions of these funds as parts of the total budget will vary according to the type of institution. Primary costs are operations—for example, salaries, maintenance, and capital expenditures. Academic administrators have resource demands that consistently exceed the funds available. Hence, it is important to analyze revenue sources and the external factors that affect them.

Academic institutions had expanded programs, faculty, staff, and physical facilities to meet the demand prior to the 1980s and were ill prepared to retrench as enrollments declined. In addition, there were radical shifts in program preferences among students. Hence, academic administrators were faced with static or declining budgets and with the need to shift resources among programs. Two academic resources that are extremely difficult, if not impossible, to shift between programs in the short run are faculty and physical facilities and equipment. These items represent a major part of any academic institution's budget. History professors are not prepared to teach engineering courses. Science buildings and equipment usually are not adaptable to accounting programs. Academic resource redistribution demands considerable lead time—for example, shifting faculty to other disciplines (retraining) and construction or adaptation of physical facilities.

The fiscal problem of most universities could be simply stated as insufficient revenues and excessive costs. Solutions to the fiscal problem, however, have to be based on a series of specific analyses regarding enrollments, tuition, endowment funds, grants, continuing education, program realignment, and capital and maintenance expenditures.

Faculty and Staff. The major cost component for academic institutions is faculty and staff salaries and benefits. Hence, annual increases in salaries and benefits have a significant impact on the institution's expenditures, and postponing any increases offers a convenient and immediate solution to a financial crisis. Such a remedy, however, affects morale and invariably results in the best and high-demand personnel leaving the university for better positions. In addition, the institution cannot attract needed personnel in the high-demand programs. Unionization of the universities is a relatively new phenomenon and can be attributed in large measure to the economic issue of salaries.

Thus, reducing salaries or deferring salary increases creates an additional problem of collective bargaining, with salary a major issue in negotiations. Universities have also tended to increase the relative number of temporary faculty, allowing more flexibility in shifting faculty hiring to high-demand programs. An increase in temporary faculty, however, creates other problems—namely, reduced research, lack of continuity and commitment, less program development, and increased faculty turnover. All these items inevitably have a negative impact on the reputation of the university and on its ability to attract students.

Faculty and staff factors represent an integral part of the CPA model and specifically involve benefits, salaries, personnel turnover, collective bargaining, temporary faculty, student-faculty ratios, and faculty and staff attitudes.

Support Functions. Since this area provides needed support for teaching and research, it is an important part of the university's operations and competes for its share of the institution's budget.

Each of the support functions should be analyzed for its contribution to the overall mission of the university. For example, a review of library services should include breadth and depth of book and periodical acquisitions and holdings, hours of operation, reference services, and prompt cataloguing. Paramount in this analysis is the extent of expenditures and how the quality and quantity of these services affect the fiscal and faculty and staff areas.

Goals and Attitudes. Strategic planning is an essential endeavor for every academic institution. It is particularly important because considerable time is needed to shift economic resources. For example, student demand tends to shift among disciplines, but a professor in a low-demand area is usually not qualified to teach in a high-demand area. With sufficient time, such resource shifts can be accomplished through retraining or attrition, but they cannot be done immediately. Hence, the institution must develop long-range strategies that allow it to shift resources as the need arises. A strategic plan encompasses the entire institution and provides for long-range planning and coordination of all activities. Successful strategic planning demands participation at every level of the organization.

Innovation and institutional image are also essential elements in fundraising and community support. All four of the areas—Fiscal, Faculty and Staff, Support Functions, and Goals and Attitudes—are interrelated, and decisions in each of the areas can have both positive and negative effects on the other areas.

Conclusion

The issue that currently confronts many academic institutions is their ability to keep the doors open for a new class, a new year, and a new generation. Universities have been confronted on almost all fronts with change, be it decreasing enrollment, cutbacks in state and federal aid, or changing attitudes and goals. The problem is one of survival. Academic institutions, because of their purpose and the nature of their operation, have no real chance to take advantage of legal protections such as bankruptcy laws. Instead, when they seek the protection of the courts, it is generally just a matter of time before those "doors to the future" are closed permanently.

Thus, it seems evident that after all the rhetoric of debate and great ideals, what can be of most help to many institutions is a framework for self-evaluation that allows the colleges to identify and define their problem areas before it is too late. The basis of the CPA model is the identification and explication of problems encountered by institutions that have or are facing the issue of their continued survival.

The importance of the CPA model is that it provides a methodology to engage in a clear and easy self-appraisal. Further, since the CPA model has a possible scoring total of 100 points, its application and results are simple and straightforward.

Clearly, the application of the CPA model is not a panacea; it does not give the strategies and methods to solve the problems. Nevertheless, its unbiased use of administrators in appraising an institution may have an even greater impact by identifying problems so that solutions can be implemented before it is too late and the doors close.

References

"A Roundup on Layoffs: Faculty Cuts and Related Actions at 17 Colleges." *The Chronicle of Higher Education,* December 8, 1982, p. 3.
Barnett, S., and O'Neill, J. P. *Colleges and Corporate Changes: Merger, Bankruptcy and Closure.* N.J.: Princeton University Press, 1981.
Biemiller, L. "A College Goes Under—But Not Without a Fight." *The Chronicle of Higher Education,* May 25, 1983, pp. 1, 6-7.
Massey, W. F., and Hopkins, D. S. P. *Planning Models for Colleges and Universities.* Palo Alto, Calif.: Stanford University Press, 1981.
"Shaw College at Detroit Seeks to Liquidate Assets." *The Chronicle of Higher Education,* March 7, 1984, p. 2.

Hal Hoverland is dean of the School of Business and Public Administration at California State University, San Bernardino.

Pat McInturff is professor of management in the School of Business and Public Administration at California State University, San Bernardino.

C. E. Tapie Rohm, Jr., is professor of information management and management in the School of Business and Public Administration at California State University, San Bernardino.

Part 2.
The Search for Solutions

After identification of the sources of organizational disequilibrium, the next logical stage in the managerial decision process is the identification and articulation of strategies. Effective solutions generally have a common set of criteria that are essential for their effectiveness. First, the proposed solution should be acceptable to those who are affected by and must implement it. Second, the solution should be compatible with the organization's mission. Third, effective solutions should not be retaliatory. Fourth, solutions should be evaluated on the basis of the present value of the costs in relation to the present value of the benefits associated with proposed changes.

The search for a solution, then, can be viewed most simply as an attempt to define and articulate a strategy that effectively and legitimately modifies those behaviors that cause dysfunctions within the organization, and that is the focus of this section.

One point that seems evident in reading the chapters of this section is the reliance on open systems and goal-oriented information linkages. Although constraints come in several forms and range from budgetary to human factors, viable solutions appear to have an underlying futuristic orientation and not just a concern for maintaining the status quo.

The final chapter of this section considers personnel packages that will take on increasing importance in labor-intensive institutions, such as academe. Clearly, the academic manager is faced with budgetary constraints, yet the university is composed of people and, whatever the solution, that fact should never be ignored.

All activities should spring from a perspective of declared institutional values, as manifested in a formal mission statement. Other institutions may glean insights from the experience of one institution's involvement with such a declaration.

The University Mission Statement: A Tool for the University Curriculum, Institutional Effectiveness, and Change

Maren E. Mouritsen

Punching and probing, a recent gaggle of commissions and reports points to a "nation at risk." The "rising tide of mediocrity," which they all challenge, I suggest is in morality and manners far more than in mathematics and manufacturing. I am certainly not the first, nor will I be the last, to suggest that the founding values and culture of the early American republic have gone unattended and neglected. In a fascinating little volume written over a half a century ago, Matthew Arnold (1925) heralded culture as the "ripe fruit of education" and educators as the "apostles of culture."

When Arnold speaks of "culture" he is thinking of the "liberal studies" that Whitney Griswold believed "are not a body of revealed truths or logical absolutes or a quantum of knowledge. They are studies designed to develop to capacity the intellectual and spiritual powers of the individual. Their aim is to make the most of man in order that he may make the most of his calling, his cultural opportunities, and his responsibilities as a citizen" (Woodring, 1985, p. 16). Arnold is emphatic that where there is not culture there is anarchy, a kind made of spiritual and moral confusion. In fact, this condition is known as *anomie:* a condition of relative normlessness or moral anarchy, a situation of crisis in which the customary norms governing the conduct of individuals have broken down, and further, a state of mind in which the individual's sense of social cohesion, the mainspring of his morale, is weakened and finally broken.

Now, fifty years and an even more powerful empirical educational philosophy later, I regret that Arnold's message has not had the impact it deserves. In fact, the ripest fruits harvested seem to be materialism, job specialization, and educators seeking to be "apostles" of moral relativism. He did not accuse empirical methods of being ineffective or inaccurate; on the contrary, it is precisely because the methods themselves became so effective that they became so seductive; concern for the methods became so great that the ends were forgotten. Would Arnold recant his fervent conviction if brought before a committee of today's university administrators, faculty, students, and citizens? Or would intellectual debate and pedantry ensue over the definition of culture and the universities' societal responsibility to cultivate the minds of the populace? Why fuss over this idea of culture anyway? (On any university campus in America, I dare say that more than one student's awareness of culture goes only as far as familiarity with Boy George and Culture Club.) What has it to do with the university curriculum, institutional effectiveness, and change? Everything—everything from the basic purpose of the university to the precepts that rule its decisions and the behavior of its "educated" people.

Culture, Values, and Institutional Integrity

No approach to education is value free. Even when none are proclaimed, values are implied. Ask whom you will, each will have a list. What is required is that individuals and institutions accept responsibility for the cultural heritage that has spawned those values. Disregard for this shared responsibility threatens not only the health of any institution but also the integrity of its social cohesion. Individuals and institutions must engage in a process of self-examination to discover the cultural foundations out of which their values are being promoted.

Values that are desirable must not be promoted in a phlegmatic manner, but strongly and confidently. It is no crime to say that you believe in something and that you seek to implement or inculcate it. It is such boldness that gives identity and purpose to an institution, an esprit de corps that can motivate unique and valuable approaches to problem solving. We must move away from the attitude that an institution can be or should be everything to every person. Rather, we should focus on developing an institutional identity and inviting people to share in and contribute to that identity.

There will always be those values that, while less concrete, are more universal in application and necessary to the ordering of any social organization, such as a university. Aristotle said, "The common good is greater and more divine than the private good" (Strauss and Cropxey, 1981, p. 77). Still, we must look for something more specific than an ambiance or setting. A declation of specific values, principles, and tenets performs several functions as an organization moves to formalize its meaning and intent. First, it defines and operationalizes choices so that an individual within the organization with particular values can find compatibility in an overarching structure. Second, a core value system that is regularly affirmed will bind the various components of an institution into a common cause and provide the basis for the development of a paradigm by which all members of the institutional community can mutually participate and develop in the more global environment. Third, it brings order so that the institution can get on with its business, rather than squandering precious time trying to make order out of chaos. Fourth, there is an intrinsic connection between individual interest in the short term and institutional morality over the long term. In this regard, a formal declaration, such as a mission statement, provides a cluster of values that can be identified and are ready for implementation and instruction.

It has been said that virtues are more often caught than taught. "Like a contagious disease, almost," William James wrote, "spiritual life passes from man to man by contact" (Perry, 1962, p. 27). If so, the context in which ideas are taught and the way they are taught have at least as much effect on students as the ideas themselves. Since education implants culture both formally and informally, this connection occurs not only in teaching but also in the behavior practiced at the institution. That is why such factors as a university's residential life, employment practices, admissions policies, investment portfolios, governance practices, curricular offerings, and overall intellectual and social atmosphere become key benchmarks in assessment of institutional intent.

The university needs to inculcate integrity with respect to its mission and translate that mission into day-to-day operations. It cannot expect more integrity from its faculty and students than it possesses or expects of itself. To the extent that the university is a faithful reproduction of its expressed culture, the faculty, staff, and students will be equipped with values that have been universally espoused and mutually accepted.

In sum, while change is inevitable, our response to it is not. We must take care to approach all change within our institutional framework with an eye toward integrating it into a coherent whole, consistent with existing values. This will verify the elements of the institution and prevent confusion or incongruity. It is also important for us to boldly proclaim and uphold our values. This will ensure an institutional identity and provide a basis for leadership in academe.

Mission Statement as a Catalyst for Change

That change takes place, both in the external and the internal environments, and impinges on the institution's regular patterns of movement goes without mention. Of crucial importance is the manner in which agents of the institution choose to respond to change. If the response is incorrect, there is a real danger not only of damaging the integrity of the institution but also of sowing confusion and distrust among its members. For this reason, careful attention must be given to how institutional agents integrate their responses to change, as it relates to the institutional mission statement.

There are both long-term and short-term effects that influence an institution and may dictate an appropriate response. For example, the recent spate of student demands for a withdrawal of university funds from investments that are related to South Africa has created a need among many colleges and universities to consider investment strategies and how they relate to institutional commitments and values. In many cases, the subsequent responses have not been made in terms of this core value system, but rather for more pragmatic and immediate reasons, such as pressures and public relations.

Whatever decision is made, it will have long-term consequences that could contribute to institutional stress. In fact, the most important aspect of such a choice may not be what is done so much as that a clear explanation of the action's relation to the institution's values and goals be made. This provides a means for people to give proper place to it within the constellations of the university. If the explanation is adequate, it will help support institutional structures, rather than undermining them. Such a strategy requires a constant and consistent effort to reaffirm and re-evaluate stated goals in relation to facts of institutional behavior as well as to the foreseeable effects and influences of current events.

It was just such a failure of proper explanation of the role of the United States government, industry, and education in world affairs that contributed to student unrest in the 1960s. While the students had legitimate concerns about the actions of the "establishment" in relation to American ideals, the "establishment" exacerbated the situation by failing to communicate a viable explanation of its actions. This failure has left tragic scars on the minds of our young. Much has been made of the disillusionment and distrust held by students of the 1960s and by subsequent generations toward institutions of all kinds. One of the saddest results may be a withdrawal of individuals into greater preoccupation with self (Astin and others, 1984; Levine, 1980).

The future will undoubtedly bring about new pressures and change agents. The shrinking of the traditional potential student population, improving secondary education, shifting needs of the economy, and changes in societal values will all have direct bearing on present ways of carrying on university activities. While some consideration can be given beforehand to changes that can be anticipated, such as those demographically induced, there will be less time to anticipate other changes, such as those that are politically or economically induced. Examining existing programs for their ability to promote their stated goals as they relate to the institution's mission statement, we are able to make clear judgments about the efficacy and fidelity of those programs in relation to those core values.

Brigham Young University: Private Values Made Public

As a private institution, Brigham Young University (BYU) is unique in American higher education. While acquiring a growing academic reputation, it is explicit about the moral and ethical standards expected of students, faculty, administrators, and staff; as a Mormon-sponsored institution, it remains for all intents and purposes independent from public funding and the attendant implications of external control. Since no other university of which I am aware possesses all three of these qualities, I see Brigham Young University as having potential to provide a unique case study regarding the role culture and values can play in an institution operating in a society that is becoming increasingly governmentalized as well as secularized.

The Mission of BYU

At the beginning of his tenure as the ninth president of BYU, Jeffrey R. Holland, (1981) extended this admonition to the faculty and staff of the university: "We want all of our resources, but especially our human resources, used in the best way possible. If someone or something is good around here, we want to support it, to foster and encourage it. . . . We have come to a time at BYU when to do some things well may require us not to do other things at all. We cannot do everything, but what we choose to do, we will do very well. Some things matter more than others to the future of BYU, and we invite you to make a case right now for what matters most to you" (p. 12). President Holland's invitation was an initial solicitation that began a university-wide effort to set forth the mission of Brigham Young University. Extreme care was taken to formulate this mission statement and the degree to which it embodies the historical and theological roots of Mormon culture.

The Mission Statement of BYU

The aspirations and attitudes of BYU's mission statement not only address the core values undergirding our educational efforts but also constitute a social norm that softens the fracturing effects of the usual academic, professional, and personal controversies and disputes present at all institutions of higher learning. These principles provide the common fund from which mutually agreed-upon educational and cultural values have been drawn.

Brigham Young University is committed by its mission statement to "assist individuals in their quest for perfection and eternal life." Explicated, this translates into instruction, programs, and services that contribute to the "balanced development of the total person." These are directed by clearly stated goals that express "moral virtues which characterize the life and teaching of the Son of God," provide broad university education, prepare individuals in areas of career choice, and encourage creative endeavor.

At BYU the curricula are developed in ways that attempt to integrate stated goals and promote the core values of the institution. This means that everything from astrophysics to zoology is taught so that the teachings of Jesus Christ are incorporated into curricula in a relevant manner. Thus, curricula and degree programs are evaluated on criteria other than their ability simply to communicate skills as an end in themselves. Training received is examined not only for its potential relevance to a useful occupation but also for its ability to engage a student in a broad search for universal values and Christian ideals. It is important, too, that any programs starting out in support of the institution's objectives do not evolve into programs that become inconsistent with institutional values.

Our athletic program, for example, has received national recognition and attention during the past few years. While this very success has the potential of engendering great enthusiasm for and identification with the institution, it also has the potential for abuse and for development of goals inconsistent with the purposes of the institution. These dangers can be guarded against by the same commitment to values and evaluations that would be applied to any other program of the university.

Our students are another influence on the structures of the university and the institutions it upholds. Today's students are hard to generalize and harder to describe. They bring a mix of values, ideals, opinions, goals, experiences, and notions of what they expect from a university education. By and large, they have lost the starry-eyed idealism or, as some would say, the naivete of preceding generations. They do have a more pragmatic sense of what can be accomplished and of effective ways of achieving their goals. The growth of student-led lobbies and community service groups has demonstrated the sophistication and capacity of today's students. This same sophistication will transfer to the classroom, where students will increasingly demand their money's worth from instruction. While we have little doubt of our ability to deliver quality products, there must be a conscious effort to relate these to relevant values. The challenge for higher education will not be in capability, but in responsibility.

Conclusion

The mission of education today must include a commitment to the retaking of the high ground of moral, spiritual, social, and intellectual leadership. This cannot be done with a haphazard and eclectic handling of change agents. If our institutions do not make clear-cut and well-explained decisions, resulting in focused efforts, we will by and large fail our responsibility and even our duty to strengthen the resolve and determination of our students to do well in this life's work. Instead, we will only reinforce the feelings of pessimism and fatalism that are already too dangerously prevalent today. History has shown that it is not the pessimist who is prepared to contribute to real solutions to society's problems, but rather the confident, directed individual who works toward a resolution of the serious issues of the day.

If institutions of higher education hope to maintain their relevance to contemporary society, they must strongly affirm their values and ideals openly and clearly. One of the greatest concerns of students today is the lack of leadership, not only from individuals but also from institutions. To many, it appears that strong leadership has been totally abdicated by many cherished institutions. But we have the leadership that higher education demands and needs; our dilemma is not an "absence of leaders but a paucity of values that will sustain them" (Guzzardi, 1980, p. 45). Religious fundamentalism and political conservatism may not be so much phenomena of profound value changes as responses to the need for clear-cut direction. Therefore, it might be wrong to assume that today's younger generation is undergoing a change in fundamental philosophical values, rather exhibiting the timeless need for mentoring and guidance.

A carefully considered and enunciated mission statement, when augmented by a conscious, informal commitment to its fulfillment, will have a forceful impact on the ability of an institution not only to maintain its integrity as a unitary structure but also to provide direction. It will induce confidence among its associates, whether they be faculty, administrators, staff, or students. By such means, the institution is able to integrate and adapt the elements of society to ensure internal consistency and to defend the integrity of the organization against external threat.

References

Arnold, M. *Culture and Anarchy.* New York: Macmillan, 1925.
Astin, A. W., and others. *The American Freshman: National Norms for 1980-1984.* Los Angeles: Cooperative Institutional Research Program, Laboratory for Research in Higher Education, Graduate School of Education, University of California, 1984.
Guzzardi, W., Jr. "The Past as Prologue: A Fabulous Fifty Years." *Fortune,* February 11, 1980.
Holland, J. R. "Virtue et Veritas." Speech given to faculty conference, Brigham Young University, Provo, Utah, September 1, 1981.
Levine, A. *When Dreams and Heroes Die: A Portrait of Today's College Student.* San Francisco: Jossey-Bass, 1980.
Perry, R. B. (Ed.). *Essay in Faith and Miracles.* New York: Meridian Books, 1962.
Strauss, L., and Cropxey, J. (Eds.). *History of Political Philosophy.* Chicago: University of Chicago Press, 1981.
Woodring, P. "The University and the Mind: Scholarship versus Culture." *Current,* February 1985.

Maren M. Mouritsen is assistant executive vice-president and dean of student life at Brigham Young University.

The allocation of scarce resources demands a planning and budgeting system that is integrated into the decision and control process.

Planning and Resource Allocation Management

Jack W. Coleman

There is a variety of evidence to suggest that the remaining years of the 1980s and the 1990s will be at least as challenging to universities as were the 1970s. Universities will continue to want to control their own destinies and to be proactive in creating and understanding their environments, as contrasted with being reactive or adaptive. At the same time, it seems apparent that they will want to introduce change, expand or enrich programs, and become involved in constructive activities in excess of financial capability. In other words, they will continue to do battle with the age-old economic problem, the allocation of scarce means to alternative ends.

Management Enhancement

Universities are generally recognizing these challenges and the importance of finding solutions to preserve, enhance, and enrich the quality of their programs without mortgaging their futures. The intuitive decision process, no matter how well intended or collegial, is slowly giving way to or being reinforced by modern scientific management methods and decision support systems.

Consequently, over the past ten to fifteen years, we have witnessed a flurry of interest by university management, whether public or private, in research and activities concerning planning, revenues, and resource allocations. For example, many resource allocation decisions have moved from internal group bargaining to cost reimbursement-based techniques, possibly incorporating zero-based budgeting needs analyses, to consideration of the more encompassing PPBS (Planning, Programming Budget System) and to strategic planning concepts. Figure 1 provides an interesting summary and perspective regarding allocation strategies (Morgan, 1984).

While these trends are encouraging, evidence seems to suggest that for many universities, these decision tools are not necessarily integrated into the management decision and control process. For example, planning may be static, and it may exist just for the sake of planning and having a mission and goals statement. Financial implications of short-term decisions may be ignored. University management, to be effective and consistent, must function within a comprehensive, integrated framework or system. It attempts to rationalize decision making by minimizing its ad hoc characteristics and by systematically taking into account benefits and costs and other implications for both the short and the long term.

Figure 1. Resource Allocation Strategies

ROOT ASSUMPTION	ALLOCATION MODEL	"OLD STRATEGIES"	"NEW STRATEGIES"	STRENGTHS	WEAKNESSES
RATIONAL CALCULATION	Goals Rational deduction	PPBS MBO	Strategic planning	Focuses on ends Relates means to ends Sense of direction	Assumption of knowledge Consensus Flexibility/ optimism
	Investment (marginal utility)	Cost/Benefit Zero Based Budget (ZBB)	Performance budgeting	Focus on results Objectivity Manageable scope	Validity of criteria Reliability of measures Ad hoc nature
	Cost Reimbursement	Performance budgeting	Marginal cost formulae	Simplicity Routinization Equity	Status quo Lack of planning
MARKET INTERACTION	Interest group bargaining	Log Rolling	Domain Defense	Political rationality Flexibility	Non- directional Status quo Tyranny of majority
	Structuring incentives	Vouchers "every tub" HMOs	Responsibility center budgeting Incentive planning	Responsiveness Competition Decision close to action	Non- directional Lack of central control Absence of real market conditions

Integrated Management System

The university management process, like all management processes, is an iterative, continuing series of activities and decisions. One significant means of minimizing chaos in decision making is to have a management process that introduces discipline, consistency, breadth of perspective, and a continuing focus on goals and objectives. Figure 2 is just such a system or set of systems. It is a closed-loop integrated management systems approach. It embraces strategic long-term planning, which of necessity forces a university to take a hard look at where it is in relation to the world about it, where it would realistically like to be at some future date, its priorities, possible trade-offs, and the development of operational and financial strategies for achieving its goals and objectives. The process must result in definable objectives, which can be translated into operational actions and lend themselves to measurement.

Figure 3 provides a possible time-phased integration of the key activities and decision points in the closed-loop management process. It is based on a public university appropriation funding process but is readily adaptable to a private university cycle as well.

Figure 2 depicts the four phases of a management cycle. Briefly, they are described here.

Phase 1, Assessment. This phase focuses on analyses of the internal and external environments, facilities, costs, and the projection of environment and university potential, which provides the background for reassessment of goals and objectives. Computer-based modeling can be a significant tool for this phase. CAMPUS and RRPM (Massey and Hopkins, 1981) are two well-known models that can simulate a variety of university scenarios over a varying time period and forecast related resource requirements. (For example, RRPM, with its induced courseload matrix, can translate enrollment projections into demand for courses, faculty, staff, and facilities. In turn, a faculty staffing model can project recruitment expectations by incorporating university policies and data concerning appointment, retention, tenure, retirement, age and rank distribution, and so forth.)

Phase 2, Strategic Planning. Utilizing the input developed in Phase 1, this phase is concerned with the reassessment and phasing of goals and objectives throughout the planning life cycle, including operational and financial strategies for their achievement. Through trade-off analyses, priorities and revenue/expenditure equilibrium are addressed. Models such as Stanford's TRADE or EDUCOM-EFPM (Massey and Hopkins, 1981) can be of great value to these analytical activities and related decisions.

Phase 3, Operational Planning. This phase focuses on the development of annual operating plans for the base year of the strategic plan. As this phase develops, the base year plan is adjusted for current budget information and evaluated again for long-term implications.

Figure 2. "X" University Management Cycle

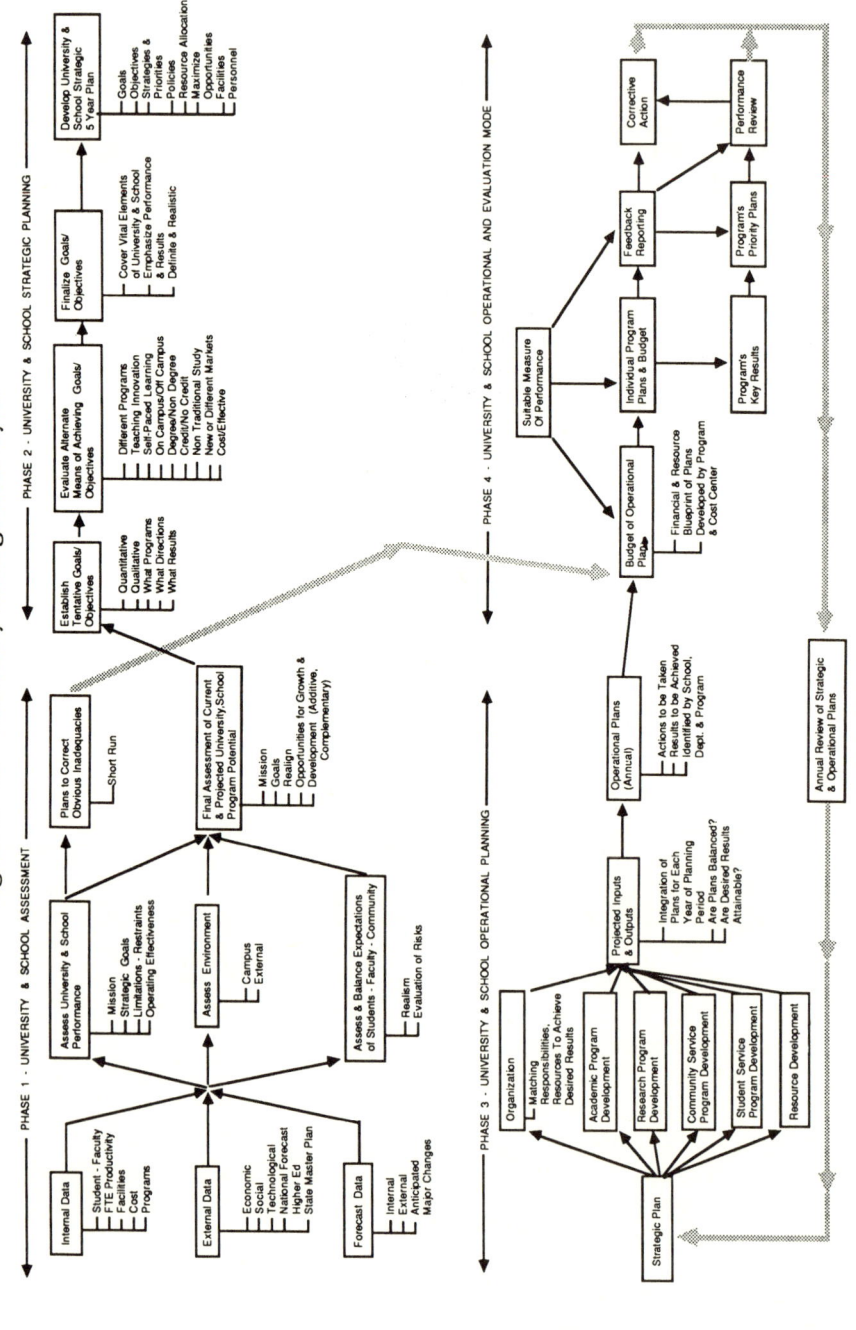

Figure 3. "X" University Strategic Plan/Program Budget/Allocation Review (A Decision-Making Device)

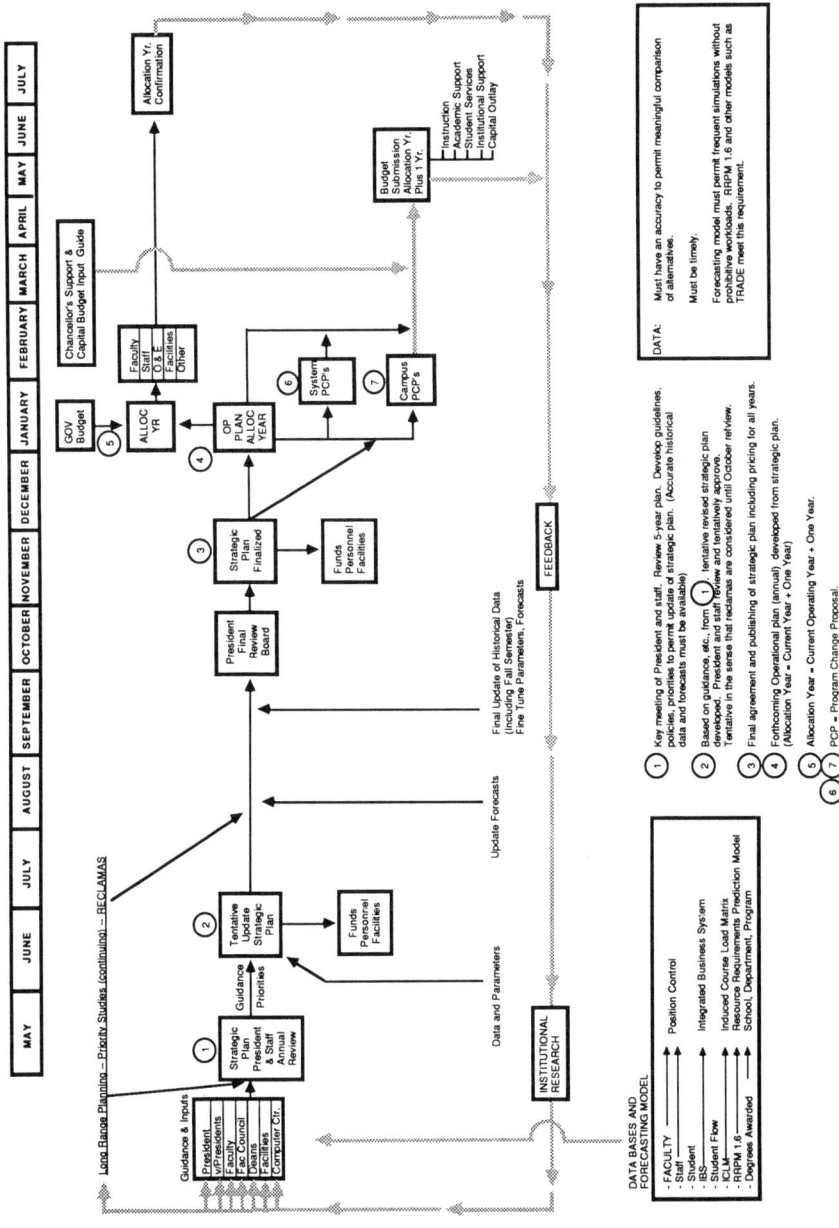

Phase 4, Operational and Evaluation Mode. This phase implements the base year of the strategic plan, including allocation of resources in conformance with the plan and monitoring of progress throughout the base year. Feedback reports provide information and data to permit operational evaluation of progress toward achieving goals and objectives, financial performance, and budget policy compliance. Performance data are introduced into the internal data banks, which support control and Phase 1 assessment.

The focal points of university management and, hence, the integrated management system are planning and budgeting, computer-based modeling, and information systems.

Planning and Budgeting

Planning and budgeting are intricately interwoven and have closely related, mutually supporting roles. Planning is an effort to determine and control the destiny of an institution. Budgeting is the pricing or costing mechanism, which develops the financial blueprint for plans. During the repetitive planning cycle reiteration, this pricing or cost mechanism exerts pressure regarding priorities, financial feasibility, and implementation insights concerning trade-offs and resource commitments and their timing. In the end analysis, planning decisions, like all decisions, must pass the test of judgment and affordability in the absolute sense, as well as in the margin. The end objective is to introduce and manage change toward long-term equilibrium between expected revenue and expenditures. The base year of the plan must reflect financial balance, while its "out years" must reflect balanced growth.

Long-term strategic planning, to be meaningful, requires long-term (dynamic) budget planning. Institutional goals and planning objectives, as well as decisions made in the short term, must be consistent with long-term financial expectations.

The planning horizon should be at least five years. Lack of resources and possibly of societal flexibilities (Lindquist, 1978) in the short term reinforce the desirability of an extended planning horizon. Universities do not change direction easily or without at least some pain. The long-term planning horizon provides opportunity for persuasive maneuvering (politicking) and acclimation of the university community to proposed, significant changes. Some would argue that all long-term planning does is provide time for the opposition to mobilize, but it also provides an opportunity to develop creative financial strategies to minimize resource implications for any one time period.

Planning and Resource Allocation Models

Planning, resource allocation, and other explicit models (formulas) are products of modern management decision concepts and techniques and of the ready availability of computers. Computer-based models are becoming an integral part of formal decision theory. Models are a vehicle by which predictions of performance of policies, actions, and processes are made. They may also be the bases of control.

The literature has been comprehensive in its coverage and analysis of concepts and major modeling efforts associated with university planning and resource allocations. There has been discussion and analysis regarding MIS (Management Information Systems), PPBS, NCHEMS' RRPM (Resource Requirements Prediction Model), the University of Toronto's CAMPUS (Campus Analytical Methods for Planning in University Systems), and Stanford's popular TRADES (interactive computer model used for budget forecasting and trade-off analysis). Each has its strengths and weaknesses, as well as supporters and critics. Regarding TRADES, Educom has developed a generalized financial planning model (EDUCOM-EFPM), which is currently being used by over seventy universities of varying size and complexity. It should be noted that neither TRADES nor EFPM inundates the user with voluminous data demands. In the absence of on-site computer capacity, EFPM can be run by making arrangements to access Cornell University's computer. Within various universities models have been embraced with varying degrees of enthusiasm. To enhance their receptivity and integration into the decision process, the following guidelines have evolved regarding the development of models (Wyatt, Emery, and Landis, 1979):

1. Modeling must be supported with staff expertise, which includes statistics, operations research, systems analysis, and modeling skills, as well as a basic understanding and knowledge of the administrative dynamics of the university.

2. Strong support of top executives is critical if the model is to be meaningfully integrated into the planning and resource allocation decision process.

3. Decision makers, to be committed to utilization of a model, must know that model. It is recommended that they be involved in its development as well as in hands-on use. (Knowledge of purpose, variables, and model control is essential.)

4. Models must strive for simplicity so as not to overpower the would-be users. The combination of mathematics and the computer tends to inhibit or exclude the generalist, while raising concerns regarding the role of quantitative versus qualitative values, as well as usefulness.

5. Models should be data-efficient, which is a function of user expectation and the resultant number of variables and parameters introduced into the model.

6. Models must produce credible and usable quantitative outputs to complement qualitative decision making. A model's credibility and usability is judged in relation to its ability to relate reasonably to the behavior of the real-world system.

Universities, by their heritage, are generous in their willingness to share their developments and accomplishments. Universities not now involved in the use of planning and resource allocation models may find it efficient to consider taking advantage of the state of the art, rather than reinventing the wheel. If this route is followed, care must be exercised to ensure that the staff and decision makers make the personal investment necessary to make the model theirs and to customize it to the particular needs of the university (Massey and Hopkins, 1981, p. 451). Without this commitment, effective integration of the model into planning and resource allocation and other decision processes is doubtful.

The combination of scientific management data needs and the computer's ability to effectively and efficiently handle and manipulate data has placed a premium on relevant, accurate, and timely data. While decisions are related to future actions and expectations, the base line for initiating the decision process is historical data. As in the management process itself, ad hoc, discrete data collection and storage files have given way to integrated information systems. For example, budget and financial data, student and faculty data, facilities data, and so forth, can each be thought of as separate systems; together, they should constitute a "system of systems." Each individual system should be evaluated in terms of its interrelationship with the total system, rather than as an independent system.

Key university data and information subsystem elements are:
1. Student data (applications, admissions, enrollment, academic, nonacademic, and so forth)
2. Faculty and staff data (position control, budget, workload, academic and nonacademic, and so forth)
3. Financial (budget and allocations, expenditures, payroll, financial aid, and so forth)
4. Facilities (land, buildings, rooms, equipment, maintenance control, and so forth)

These data provide the basis for analytic studies, development of program and cost relationships, cost behavioral patterns, and forecasting the future.

Conclusions

The introduction of modern scientific management processes and techniques can and does provide university administrators with valuable planning and resource allocation insights and enhances the decision process. To optimize effectiveness, there needs to be an overall integrated closed-loop management system, which incorporates assessment, strategic planning, dynamic budgeting, operational planning, and a feedback and control process regarding actual operations and subsequent planning. It is critical that planning be complemented by dynamic, long-term budgeting, so that the focus of management is on long-term equilibrium between expected revenues and expenditures.

Computer-based models can be of significant help to university managers in framing scenarios and resulting policy and priority decisions. For effective modeling, there must be specific staff expertise, strong executive support and knowledge of the models, and output credibility. Models do not replace management judgment; properly used, they enhance that judgment.

References

Lindquist, J. *Strategies for Change.* Berkeley, Calif.: Pacific Soundings Press, 1978.
Massey, W. F., and Hopkins, D. S. P. *Planning Models for Colleges and Universities.* Stanford, Calif.: Stanford University Press, 1981.
Morgan, A. "New Financial Strategies for Higher Education." In R. Wetson (Ed.), *Selected Proceedings of Annual Conference on Higher Education.* Tucson: Center for the Study of Higher Education, University of Arizona, 1984.
Wyatt, J. P., Emery, J. C., and Landis, C. P. (Eds.). *Financial Planning Models: Concepts and Case Studies in Colleges and Universities.* Princeton, N.J.: Educom, 1979.

Jack W. Coleman is vice-president for academic affairs and former dean of the School of Business and Economics at California State University, Fullerton.

The use of a systematic constraint removal process should be an integral part of change strategies in higher education and should be incorporated into the decision process.

A System for Constraint Removal

Reese Parker

Constraints: Context and Conditions

In our institutions, problem recognition implies that alternative solutions will be generated and that action will be taken to solve the problem or at least to reduce its negative effects. This idea is central to the social compact between higher education and the society that supports it. Colleges and universities are resistant to change, as are other established social institutions. We enjoy the traditions of free and virtually unlimited debate, broad participation in the decision process, and systematic investigation of problems and alternate solutions by our internal constituencies.

As public institutions, colleges and universities are visible to and influenced by legislatures, lay boards, single-interest groups, alumni, and other external constituencies, which do not always share our valued intellectual traditions. Traditionally, discovering that something is not true, effective, viable, valid, and why that is the case is valued equally with discovering that something is true or effective among members of the internal constituencies. The tradition of controversy surrounding the search for truth and expansion of knowledge and skills is institutionalized in higher education and is frequently a point of contention among various constituencies.

This abbreviated description of the context in which higher education operates can be expanded to include such notions as the increasing demands that society is placing upon higher education and the increasing scrutiny its appropriations receive; that higher education is a major contributor to the knowledge explosion and technological change, which in effect force citizens to live with greater ambiguity and increasing rates of change; and that these factors are more likely to intensify than they are to dissipate in the future.

Listing these factors reveals a reality about change and higher education that is central and increasingly important for our continued effectiveness. Any strategy that we undertake to improve various aspects of our operation, any proactive change that we implement to take advantage of emerging opportunities or to avoid negative effects from emerging societal trends, any growth strategy we pursue to expand our mission to better serve society faces immediate constraints (Drucker, 1977). The conflicting demands, values, modes of operation, and goals that can be easily inferred from the conditions listed virtually guarantee that any change strategy will encounter difficulties that decrease or hinder its effective implementation (constraints) and thereby limit its ultimate positive effect (Conner, 1980).

Validate this proposition for yourself. We all store visual and auditory images. Close your eyes and engage the tape of the last time the core curriculum was changed at your institution. Play back the last fee increase, the last new program establishment effort, the last proposal to create a research and development unit, the last big push to reach out and accommodate the needs of an underserved segment of society. Note the objections, rational and irrational, as your tape reveals administrative, faculty, student, staff, alumni, state board, legislative, and special-interest images. Note that strengths and reasons for pursuing the change cited by one constituency are judged to be weaknesses and reasons for not pursuing the change by another. Visualize clearly that the effects sought go too far for some and do not go far enough for others, while still others doubt that the strategy is sufficient to achieve the proposed effects. As more aspects of the proposed change emerge in the lively debate, watch the constituencies undergo fragmentation. Rejoice in the images of polarization of subgroups around a single issue or aspect associated with the proposed change. As your tape winds down, remember your evaluation of the change planned versus the change attained, or of shelving the whole matter and returning to the drawing boards. Remember that you are certain to encounter lingering dissatisfaction with whatever happened from at least a dozen sources during the next twenty-four hours.

The constraint removal process suggested here is designed to make such a tape review a more pleasant experience, filled with a higher portion of pleasant images. The process suggests that the systematic identification, analysis, and removal or reduction of constraints and their effects be an integral part of any change strategy. Doing this increases the likelihood of success in the change effort and reduces the long-term negative effects of existing constraints (Smith, 1963). Effective use of the process assumes that managers of change are knowledgeable of their operating contexts and of constituencies' values and interests and that they wish to gain positive effects from the change process, as well as from the change itself.

Constraint Characteristics

Constraints can be described in terms of three characteristics: area of affect, source, and location. The area of affect is that part of the organization where the constraint exerts (or will exert) negative influence on the proposed change. The source is the reason that the constraint exists. The location of the constraint is the entity that gives power to the constraint.

Suppose a college or university proposes alternatives to the traditional classroom model for instructional delivery, to better serve students who are remote from the main campus. Concerns about accountability and student achievement (area of affect) may emerge in the faculty (location) because of a mistrust of alternative delivery systems (source). An administrative reorganization proposal may draw fire from the institutional or state governing board (location) because of a policy or rule (source) requiring a minimum number of subunits in a span of authority in order to receive budget allocations (resource allocation is the area of affect) from state appropriations.

The emphasis on managers of change being and becoming more knowledgeable about their constituencies to effectively use constraint removal processes can be illustrated in both examples. The faculty's publicly announced objection to the effect of alternative delivery systems upon accountability for student achievement is initially identified as the constraint. The manager may begin a strategy to change faculty attitudes toward alternative delivery systems. In the process, it becomes obvious that the objection is not that attitude but rather the attitude toward the administrative unit or administrator charged with implementing the alternative program.

Presentation of a strong case to the governing board, clearly demonstrating the economic and educational benefits of reorganization, should be an effective constraint removal strategy for the situation described. It establishes a valid rationale for making an exception to the policy. However, the change manager may discover that the real constraint is that the most influential member of the board is opposed to any change that would increase the resources available to this institution. The real constraint is attitudinal, not policy-based, and the appropriate removal strategy would be political (exerting influence upon other board members), rather than informational.

A Constraint Removal Process

A four-step constraint removal process is proposed here. It is a general procedural model that must be adapted for specific use. The model promotes integration of constraint removal efforts with any strategy. It enables the manager of change to operate from a research-supported logical base, rather than from an intuitive one. It promotes prior identification of blocks and blockers in proposed changes. It identifies the types of efforts educational change literature identifies as being most likely to succeed under differing conditions (Parker, 1971).

In the description of the constraint removal process that follows, directions and descriptions focus on the role of the change manager, that individual ultimately responsible for the change strategy. The change manager holds responsibilities in a community of experts, whose skills and knowledge should be used throughout the process of constraint removal. The model assumes that the change manager will use the best information sources available in performing change and constraint removal. Meaningful participation in these processes by members of the varied constituencies of the college or university is strongly recommended as conducive to effective and productive change effects.

Step One: Identify Area Affected

The change manager identifies the areas of action (those affected by the constraints) in the first step. This step focuses attention on the goal that is most likely to be adversely affected in the change strategy. The model presented offers eight classifications of area of actions: planning and resource use, human talent use, technology use, curriculum/instruction, space and facilities use, time use, accountability/student achievement, and social psychological factors.

Step Two: Identify Constraint Source

Step two requires identification of the sources of constraints, the causes or reasons for their existence. Four categories are used to identify constraint sources: competencies, attitude, material, policy. Competencies are constraining when success of the proposed change requires skills that are unavailable in the institution or present in insufficient quantity or quality, or when highly skilled persons are so assigned that their skills are not available for use in the change strategy. If a university establishes a foundation to seek additional resources for research and development but has no skilled fundraisers or has assigned its best fundraiser to the responsibility of athletic director or has goals that exceed the capabilities of available grantspersons and fundraisers, then it faces a constraint in the competency category.

Attitudes are constraint sources when they represent opposition to necessary or desired changes. Such opposition constrains the availability and effective use of resources. Availability is restricted when negative attitudes impel less than full participation in the change strategy. Use is restricted when persons are excluded from the change strategy for fear that their opposition will affect supporters' contributions. For example, a college decides to develop several interdisciplinary courses in its required core, when it is forced to release several faculty members because of funding cutbacks. These professors are the only experts in their particular disciplines. Their major role has been to provide richness and breadth to general education offerings. Interdisciplinary courses were determined to be the most effective means of preserving some of their contributions. However, the dean of arts and sciences is totaly opposed to interdisciplinary courses and becomes an active and influential blocker. While the change manager may be tempted to remove the holder of the attitude, it seems more productive to focus on neutralizing the effects of the attitude, given the upheaval existent in the institution as a result of the layoffs.

Material constraints are easiest to identify because they consist of the absence or shortage of necessary machinery, equipment, structures, consumables, and so forth. If the material is not present in the system, then the constraint concerns availability. If the material is present but is being employed so that alternate use is prohibited, the constraint is use. Differing material constraints require varied removal strategies.

Policy constraints consist of those regulations, rules, and executive policies that affect resources by restricting their availability and use in the organization. These are usually evident in state statutes, board regulations, institutional policy and procedure handbooks, catalogues, and presidents' policy statements.

Step Three: Identify Constraint Location

The third step in the constraint removal process is to identify the location of the constraint. The location is that force giving power to the constraint and enabling it to threaten the success of a change strategy. Five classifications of constraint location are used in this process: constituted boards and bodies, students, faculty and staff, authority hierarchies, and specific external constituencies. Constituted boards and bodies include the legislature, regents, accrediting agencies, and so forth. Authority hierarchies include administrators, the executive branch, and courts. Faculty and staff include individuals, such faculty governance bodies as curriculum committees, and faculty senates. Specific external constituencies include alumni, corporations, political lobbies, businesses, campus neighbors, professional organizations, and civic organizations.

After step three, the constraint is fully described in terms of area of affect, source, and location. This enables use of the matrix in Figure 1.

Figure 1. Constraint Removal Matrix

AREA AFFECTED

SOURCE	PLANNING AND RESOURCE ALLOCATION	HUMAN TALENT USE	TECHNOLOGY USE	CURRICULUM CONCERNS	SPACE AND FACILITIES	TIME USE	STUDENT ACHIEVEMENT AND ACCOUNTABILITY	SOCIO-PSYCHOLOGICAL FACTORS
COMPETENCY	2 3 5 7 9	2 3 5 7 9	2 3 5 7 9	2 3 5 7 9	1 2 3 5	1 2 3 9	2 3 5 7 9	2 3 5 7 9
ATTITUDE	1 7 8 9 10	1 3 7 8 9 10	1 7 8 9	1 7 8 9	1 7 8 9	1 7 8 9	1 7 8 9	1 7 8 9
MATERIAL	1 2 3 5 6	1 2 3 4 5 6	1 2 3 4 5 6	1 2 3 5 6	1 2 3 4 5 6	1 2 3	1 2 3 5 9 10	1 2 3 4 5 6
POLICY	6 8	6 8	6 8	6 8	6 8	6 8	6 8	6 8

STRATEGIES
1. REBUDGET
2. REALLOCATE
3. REORGANIZE
4. RESTRUCTURE
5. PROVIDE RESOURCES
6. TAKE REQUIRED ACTION
7. RECRUIT
8. PUBLIC RELATIONS
9. RETRAIN
10. REWARD/MOTIVATE

LOCATION	APPROPRIATE STRATEGY
A. STAFF	1 2 3 5 7 8 9 10
B. CONSTITUTED BOARD	6 8
C. AUTHORITY HIERARCHY	4 6 8
D. STUDENT BODY	1 2 3 5 7 8 9 10
E. EXTERNAL CONSTITUENCY	7 8 10

The matrix identifies ten categories of alternate strategies for constraint removal. It classifies strategies that the organizational change literature suggests as effective for specific combinations of areas affected and sources of constraints. The boxed table below the matrix identifies feasible strategies by constraint location, using the same literature as a basis for the relationships displayed.

Suppose the change manager identifies the area affected to be planning and resource allocation, source to be attitude, and location to be some specific external constituency—for example, alumni. The matrix lists five strategies at the "attitude/planning and resource allocation" intersection and three feasible strategies for the external constituency location in the box below the matrix. The two lists have three strategies in common: recruit, public relations, and reward/motivate. The process has generated development by the change manager.

For example, a plan to move resources from supporting a traditional set of homecoming activities to supporting expansion of a program can easily raise the ire of alumni (location), whose attitude of support (source) for homecoming activities has the effect of blocking the planned resource allocation (area affected). The in-common alternate strategies for this constraint description suggest that the change manager "recruit" alumni to support the proposed reallocation of funds or do "public relations" (compile, communicate, and advocate favorable information about the proposed change) with the blockers themselves, or "reward/motivate" alumni for supporting the change (give alumni visibility and sincere recognition for their support of the expanded program; use resources for an alumni chair in the program; give alumni scholarships to qualified students in the program who are screened and nominated by an alumni committee).

The user of the constraint removal process will note that Figure 1 conveys an image of a greater number of alternative strategies for faculty/staff and student body locations and for competency and material sources than for other characteristics. This reflects the status of educational and organizational change literature, not the relative difficulty of addressing constraints with these characteristics. We simply know more about promoting effective change in students, faculty/staff, competencies, and material aspects of our organizations than we do about others addressed in this constraint removal process.

If a university decides to expand its union building, using a bond to be retired by increased student fees for the finance strategy, student opposition to the fee increase (not the expansion) is almost certain. While student governments are usually supportive of such financing for needed change, some segments of the student body (commuting students) often oppose them. The constraint location in this case is "student body," the area affected is "planning and resource allocation," and the source is "attitude."

The source (by area affected) cell of the matrix in Figure 1 contains five plausible strategies, student body location contains eight, and the two sets intersect on five: rebudget, recruit, public relations, retrain, and reward/motivate. Retrain is not feasible in this situation. The change manager can choose among finding another way to finance the expansion (rebudget), convincing the opposition that the benefits of expansion are more valid than the attitude of opposition, recruiting student support from other segments of the student body, or dedicating some part of the expansion space (reward/motivate) specifically to the use of commuting students (locker space, car pool board, off-campus student ombudsman).

Step Four: Strategy Selection

Completing the previous steps results in a list of viable alternative strategies, which the change manager should judge to be feasible or unfeasible for the particular context. Next, the likely consequences (positive and negative) of using each strategy should be projected. The options remaining for consideration should be those with the highest ratios of positive to negative projected consequences.

At this point, the change manager may decide to delay implementation of the whole strategy because the constraint analysis produces only unfavorable positive-to-negative projected consequence ratios. This represents a positive aspect of the constraint removal process. It prevents the institution from pursuing probable no-win change strategies. Further, the analysis should have identified conditions by location, source, and area of affect, which need to be improved before implementation of any proposed change. If the institution must proceed with the change regardless of unfavorable consequence ratios, at least the change managers will know how many shields to purchase and how to arrange them to minimize bodily harm! In addition, the process identifies the targets for action in a loss-minimization strategy, which should be instituted.

Multiple Complex Constraints

As solidarity organizations and social institutions, public colleges and universities are critical points on the continuum of social change. We lead, resist, follow, impel, and reflect the changes which affect the larger society. We are a focal point, where many conflicting goals and interests of varied constituencies merge, especially when we implement substantial change in our operations to deal with effects of emergent societal trends.

Such changes as limiting enrollments, closing traditional programs, opening high-cost, high-need, high-risk, low-output graduate or research programs, and substantially changing athletic budgets produce multiple and complex constraints. What is the change manager to do in that situation, especially if the institution is in a "must change" mode?

The process should be used in the multiple complex constraint environment with several important additional guidelines. First, analysis of areas affected must be more carefully done so that strategy selection will focus on the goals of the change. Second, after step three, determine whether the consequences analysis indicates need for gradual change or for a comprehensive strategy with a short timeline for successful change. Third, the change manager must maintain coherence in the application of the constraint removal strategy. Fourth, diverse strategies must contain frequent, formal feedback mechanisms from implementation effects. This ensures that further constraints will not be created by constraint removal efforts and that those efforts will not negatively affect the consequence analysis ratio of other strategies (Lawrence and Lorsch, 1969).

Among these guidelines, maintaining coherence in constraint removal strategies is critical. The process requires focusing diverse strategies on desired positive results or goals. The change manager will make decisions about the sequencing of activities, priorities of goals to be achieved and protected, and relative energy to be allocated to various constraint removal activities, on the basis of knowledge of specific situations. In making those decisions, coherence in the overall strategy must be maintained to avoid negative impact.

Use Constraint Removal to Cope with Chaos

As solidarity organizations and social institutions in an enviroment of interrelated rapid social change, increasing demands, and proportionately shrinking resources, public colleges and universities find that change-oriented decisions are almost always contingency decisons (Greenwood, 1965). The obvious nature of this statement is reflected in perceptions of leaders in higher education, who sometimes remark cynically that the contemporary interval for long-range strategic planning is a fiscal year, at best, and four hours, at least, or that crisis and battlefield management are the most frequently occurring styles, and deciding to change the color of parking stickers can adversely affect the construction schedule of the new science center. The use of a systematic constraint removal process as an integral part of change strategies in higher education is highly appropriate to the decision environment. It aids in the identification and description of constraints; generates alternative strategies from a logical, research-literature base; forewarns the change manager of potential problem areas; and is more efficient and more likely to promote successful change than are trial-and-error, intuitive approaches. In times judged to be chaotic, any paradigm that increases the probability of productive successful change should be included in the decision making of leaders of higher education.

References

Conner, P. E. *Organization: Theory and Design.* Chicago: Science Research Associates, 1980.
Drucker, P. F. *People and Performance: The Best of Peter Drucker on Management.* New York: Harper & Row, 1977.
Greenwood, W. F. *Management and Organization Behavior Theories.* Chicago: Southwestern, 1965.
Lawrence, P. R., and Lorsch, J. W. *Developing Organizations: Diagnosis and Action.* Reading, Mass.: Addison-Weseley, 1969.
Parker, R. *Toward a System of Constraint Removal.* Tallahassee: The Evaluation Training Center, Florida State University, 1971.

Smith, B. O. "The Anatomy of Change." *National Association of Secondary School Principals Bulletin*, 1963, *47*, 7-8.

Reese Parker is dean of the School of Professional Studies at Lewis-Clark State College.

There are practical steps that educational institutions can take now to enhance self-reliant employees, employees who will provide productivity instead of problems and create organizational excellence.

The Human Factor for Optimal Solutions

Lin Bothwell

There are many theoretical models that have been developed to aid practitioners in analyzing and managing academic organizations and systems. These models have included behavioral, interpersonal, transactional, bureaucratic, resource expending, and political facets. For the person who wishes to be successful in leading and managing an educational institution, some understanding of each of these models is useful.

Choosing among the many ways of looking at your organization is important. More important is to prioritize those approaches that will be most appropriate to your understanding and management of your organization. The way you look at the problems and challenges that confront you will determine those areas that will receive your energy and resource expenditures. That which you define as your problem will in fact become your problem.

The Challenges of Educational Management

Several leading writers on management and leadership have referred to educational institutions as unmanageable. This view was so prevalent when I was doing my doctoral work at Harvard in the early 1970s that I researched it in some detail and reported it in an unpublished monograph.

It is not my purpose here to repeat the content and findings of that paper, but only to indicate that the research and analysis showed that most of the significant challenges facing educational managers and leaders resided in the human resource realm.

During the subsequent decade, the body of literature has mounted to verify that people are an organization's greatest asset and in many cases a significant liability. Your people are the key source of good news (productivity, esprit de corps, creativity, service, and problem solutions) and of challenges (absenteeism, turnover, employee sabotage, negativism, problem creation). The focus here will be on the positive; I will show that the "human factor" can lead to high-leverage, optimal solutions to organizational problems. People, properly managed, can go a long way toward coping with chaos.

Organizational Philosophers View Excellence in the 1980s

There is an ongoing intellectual revolution in how we look at and think about where people work, as well as concern with how those people and places will be affected by the broad waves of societal change that are sweeping over us.

Naisbitt (1982) has identified and documented a number of important macro changes that will affect people and where and how they work over the next two decades. Without restating those ten major trends, I have excerpted a number of specific changes he identifies.

1. We are becoming an "information society." There will be great emphasis over the next several decades on careers related to the collection, analysis, and dissemination of information. This will affect the types of programs emphasized in secondary and higher education institutions. It will also affect the way those institutions are staffed and managed.

2. There is a move toward "high tech/high touch." As technology and especially computers and VCRs proliferate, there will of necessity be an expanding need for human and humane careers and concepts. These will expand in the curriculum and, as the institution reflects the larger society, need to be built into the administrative structure of the organization. With more computer-based management and video training will come expanded emphasis on employee morale, employee recognition, managing the organizational culture, and human resource planning and development.

3. There will be a shift from institutional help to self-help. Professions and programs that stress self-reliance, how-to skills, and the development of high self-esteem will flourish. Institutions will want to provide their employees with benefits that create not dependency but self-sufficiency.

4. There will be less emphasis on hierarchies and more on networking. The formal organization will decline in importance, while the informal will ascend. Programs will aim at teaching communication and

interpersonal skills that can take advantage of this trend. The institution will want to foster horizontal linkages among employees, flexible office space and work hours, multiple bosses and roles, decentralized decision making, and the encouragement of employee suggestions and innovation.
   5. All of this will strengthen the trend from centralization to decentralization.

Naisbitt has highlighted these and other significant social and cultural trends that are sweeping over us. Educational institutions will want to be on the leading edge of the waves, not trying to swim upstream.

Peters and Waterman (1982) examine business organizations, but many of the qualities of organizational management, administration, and culture would apply with equal force to educational institutions that are concerned with achieving excellence. Specifically, they found that organizations that consistently perform excellently and profitably have some of the following characteristics:

1. They have a bias toward action. They do not get caught up in "analysis paralysis" but operate on the basis of "ready, aim, fire."
2. They encourage autonomy and entrepreneurship. The employees are encouraged to take risks and to be innovative and creative.
3. Organizational values and culture are maintained by personal and enthusiastic attention from top management.
4. The structure of the organization is kept simple and lean, and top staffs are kept small by design.
5. They employ "simultaneous loose-tight properties." They are a paradoxical combination of centralization and decentralization. They keep tight control of things that are truly important and stay extremely loose about everything else.
6. They view their people as their most important asset. They practice "productivity through people" and put energy and resources into the "care and feeding" of their employees.

These standards, and others developed by Peters and Waterman, can be used as a yardstick by organizations, as a test of commitment to excellence and productivity.

Deal and Kennedy (1982) have raised our awareness of the importance of understanding and managing corporate culture. Here, the role of the human factor in achieving organizational solutions can be clearly seen. The very best strategic plan is only as good as it implementation by the members of the organization, and the quality of this implementation is influenced and shaped by the corporate culture.

Think of an IBM or a 3M in the corporate world, or a Harvard or a Stanford in the academic world, and then think of those organizations significantly less successful than these models of excellence. Compare and contrast on the basis of how contributions are encouraged and acknowledged, how problems of staff are treated, how decisions are made, how plans are implemented and reviewed, and how leadership is demonstrated, and you will see the clear differences.

Naisbitt, Peters and Waterman, and Deal and Kennedy have pointed the way toward human solutions to organizational problems in the 1980s. These management writers and others show us with imagination and force the critical role people play in determining the success of an organization and whether it will survive, thrive, and excel in the decades ahead.

Approaches to Self-Reliant Employees and Organizational Excellence

Managing for excellence in the 1980s and beyond requires organizations and their leaders to be clear about what they can do for the people and what their people can and should do for themselves. Then the leader of vision and courage will move forward and do it. Let me suggest several organizational thrusts for your consideration. If you are not doing some of these things, consider starting; if you are doing some of them now, consider ways of doing them better.

Engage in a thoughtful examination of your organization's culture. What was the original purpose and mission of your system, institution, or department? Is it living up to that mission? Has the mission changed, or should it, to match changing societal forces? Are actions of groups and individuals evaluated and rewarded in light of that mission? Is the work climate conducive to successfully accomplishing that mission? These questions and others like them may seem mundane, but they are the stuff that organizational excellence is made of. The leading institutions consistently ask hard questions, redirect, and focus on making their strengths productive.

Create a climate and supporting practices that nurture creativity, contributions, responsible choices and actions, and personal growth. People thrive where they have a chance to make real contributions, and thriving people produce thriving institutions. Ask yourself what is being rewarded by the system, by you. What, in the challenges your institution faces, requires not just a contribution but real creativity? Is decision making decentralized? Do others feel responsible for producing results relative to the mission and goals? What provides people with an opportunity to develop, grow, expand, see new options, try new things, and reach new heights? If you think that is not possible in your organization, then think some more. This is part of your responsibility, contribution, creativity, and growth.

Expand the quantity and quality of your programs and opportunities for training, development, and continuing education. Organizations that have taken on the charge of educating and training members of the broader society often do a poor job of educating, training, and developing their own faculty, administrators, and staff. Educational organizations have always been ten to twenty years behind their business counterparts in providing their people with an opportunity to learn and grow.

Look at what your organization is doing or not doing. Recognize that skills training, education, management development, and career development are not the same things (Bothwell, 1983). People need an opportunity to learn more, things both job-related and non-job-related. People need an opportunity to expand and practice new techniques and develop them into skills. People need sources for personal introspection, for developing their talents in dealing with others, and for refining those broader qualities that make us uniquely human.

If your feeling is that some of what I have just suggested does not belong in your world of work, ask yourself why these approaches have worked so well in the excellent organizations. How would an employee feel toward an organization that provided these opportunities? Businesses talk of a "feeling of family." Does that exist in your system or institution? If not, why not? What could be done to create it?

Rightly or wrongly, the places where people work have become major sources of benefits. These benefits now account for about 36 percent of the organization's costs of compensating employees. What are the best, most essential benefits for enhancing the human factor? How can you get the most from providing those benefits, and how can certain benefits actually reduce benefit costs?

First, you need benefits that provide for employee protection and security. These can include medical insurance, disability insurance, life insurance, financial planning, and separation "cushions," should there be reductions in force. Second, you need benefits that help employees deal with problems and distractions. These can include employee assistance programs, wellness programs, counseling, and legal assistance. Third, you need benefits that provide for employee development and recognition. These can include educational assistance, skills training, management development, corporate education, and service awards programs. Finally, you need benefits that help your employees provide for a secure and stimulating future. These include career planning, a pension program, preretirement planning, and the newest program, life planning, which provides for the future, enhances existing programs, and increases employee morale while expanding self-reliance and breaking the "entitlement benefit" habit.

Life planning programs are among the newest and most interesting of employee benefits. They have grown out of the preretirement planning movements of the 1970s and early 1980s. While these programs made an important contribution to preparing employees financially and socially for a secure, rewarding retirement, they were aimed at and provided to those employees who were from one to five years away from retirement. The comment most often heard about these programs was "Why weren't we given this information twenty years ago, when we could really have done something about it?"

The need was thus created for a program that would reach

employees in the thirty-five to fifty-five age range and provide them with usable planning information in the financial, physical, and personal development areas. This led to a second development in life planning, an expanded focus over existing preretirement programs. It became clear that employees, all of us, need to see the big picture of our lives. We need to view ourselves in terms of the financial, physical, social, intellectual, emotional, spiritual, and recreational aspects of our lives and to see how those aspects correlate with corporate programs in financial planning, wellness, training, counseling, education, preretirement and career planning, company recreation, and employee assistance. A comprehensive life planning program provides this view of life and an umbrella approach to understanding company benefits.

A good life planning program will also prepare an employee for the future by teaching self-reliance. Attitudes need to be changed, and employees need to understand that government and employers are no longer going to provide a secure future as an entitled benefit. The employee will come to be grateful to you for providing consciousness-raising and the information and techniques to make self-reliance a reality.

The organization that sponsors a life planning program for its staff will send two important and seemingly paradoxical messages to its employees: First, we care about you, and we put our money where our mouth is (caring) by providing a program that helps you solve current problems and prepare intelligently for the future. Second, you must take the responsibility for your own future, for there are things we cannot (and in some cases should not) do for you.

Conclusion

There is much that the educational sector of our society can learn from the business community. While educational institutions differ from business corporations in some important ways, they have much in common and in fact are more alike than different. Your challenge is to become one of the excellent organizations, so that you do not just survive to but actually thrive through the year 2000.

References

Bothwell, L. *The Art of Leadership*. Englewood Cliffs, N.J.: Prentice-Hall, 1983.
Deal, T. E., and Kennedy, A. A. *Corporate Cultures*. Reading, Mass.: Addison-Wesley, 1982.
Naisbitt, J. *Megatrends: Ten New Directions Transforming Our Lives*. New York: Warner, 1982.
Peters, T. J., and Waterman, R. H., Jr. *In Search of Excellence*. New York: Harper & Row, 1982.

Lin Bothwell is the chairman and founder of Stonebridge Institute, Inc., a corporation that assists organizations in preparing their employees physically, legally, and financially for the future.

Part 3.
Implementation

Probably one of the most ignored areas of decision making by managers has been implementation. Historically, implementation has been an assumption of the decisional process. It was assumed that once the problem is identified and the solution defined and articulated, it would automatically be implemented. However, as is now obvious, the imposition of solutions means a proposed modification of behavior within the organization. This, in turn, creates uncertainty and the alteration of existing structures. These changes are often opposed, ignored, or altered by those who are essential to the solution's implementation.

The following chapters make clear the importance of an effective implementation strategy for achieving the resolution of disequilibrium and fostering growth and viability for the organization. Although each of the distinguished authors of the first three chapters in this section focuses on the budgetary function, it becomes very clear that open, positive communication linkages and human relations development are crucial to carrying out the chosen strategies, policies, and solutions.

The final chapter in this section looks at the future role of computers and information management in the administration of institutions of higher education.

The planning and budgeting process must be integrated into the decision making process of the university and include broad constituent participation.

The Planning-Budgeting Process: Planning as the Basis for Resource Decisions

Neil S. Bucklew, Daniel J. Smith

Planning and budgeting are integrated processes. Planning is the systematic process of determining directions for institutional progress. Budgeting is the key management activity designed to implement an institution's plans. Budgeting must reflect priority judgments in the life of the institution, as defined through its planning efforts. Each institution needs to develop a planning-budgeting process that fits its particular tradition and expectations.

Characteristics of an Effective Planning-Budgeting Process

It is possible to identify some major characteristics or qualities of an effective planning-budgeting system. These qualities do not guarantee success in the establishment of a process but should prove useful. The first quality is to establish a climate of understanding and acceptance for the implementation of a planning-budgeting system. This involves work with the constituent groups of the campus in order to gain their understanding and commitment. Faculty, staff, and students need to understand the advantages of a planning-budgeting process and be committed to their role in that activity. The governing board of the institution must also be committed to the process. It is important to assure board members that the process will not erode their ultimate responsibility for governance and general institutional policy. Nevertheless, they should understand the working system if they are to respond favorably to the recommendations generated from the planning-budgeting activity.

The planning-budgeting process needs to be comprehensive to be effective. The term *comprehensive* refers to the institution-wide nature of decisions. An effective process is concerned with program developments, both academic and administrative. This is the key element in effective planning and requires substantial time and effort. Developing a campus-wide understanding of program development and needs is imperative. It must be a dynamic process if the results are to ensure a vital university, but an understanding of program priorities is only the beginning of effective planning. Those understandings must then be applied to a wide range of fiscal decisions, staffing patterns, and campus physical developments. Partial planning in a university is rarely successful. The relationships of staffing, space, and dollar resources are critical. It is not feasible to pursue program priorities if major aspects of campus decisions are handled separately from the planning-budgeting process. Another aspect of the comprehensive quality of planning is that no part of the campus should be excused from involvement. Although academic program development is obviously at the heart of an institution's programs, it is important to include the full range of administrative programs as well.

Another basic quality of an effective planning-budgeting process is ensuring a long-term perspective. Without such a perspective, the process can quickly become a crisis form of decision making, which always views items on a one-year or shorter basis. Although short-term decisions are an inherent part of planning, it is important to place them in the context of a three- to five-year set of priorities and directions.

The last quality that needs to be present in an effective planning-budgeting process is a clear administrative commitment. Administrative responsibility takes various forms. The first is to make a definite time commitment to the process. The second is to assume the responsibility of stating, both on and off campus, a vision for the institution's development, including major themes and directions that reflect the tradition and consensus of the institution. The administration must show through its actions that it is willing to link major decisions in the life of the university to the aspirations and goals developed through the planning process.

University of Montana—A Case Description

The University of Montana is one of a number of institutions in the United States that has implemented a formal planning-budgeting process. In the case of the University of Montana, the planning process was introduced in 1981 and is now in its fifth cycle of annual planning activity.

The university publishes, on an annual basis, a document describing the planning process and schedule, major themes and directions for program development at the institution, and items necessary for implementation of planning activity (for example, planning instructions, planning schedules, and a section dealing with general assumptions influencing and creating a context for decision making at the university).

The themes and directions for planning have been developed through a dynamic series of activities. In the early stages of the planning process, the president of the university identified fourteen major themes for the 1980s. These proposed themes were shared broadly on the campus and put in final form only after a thorough critique. As the planning activities proceeded, it became clear that it was important to develop a refined statement of those goals. Again, the president was responsible, after consultation, for identifying five select areas for special focus and attention in the years immediately ahead. Those five areas were shared with the campus through an annual convocation address. A special task force, headed by faculty members at the university, was responsible for suggesting strategic steps to be pursued by the university in each of these five areas: student enrollment maintenance, communication development, general education, select program development, and research and creative activities development. Within the context of these five strategic areas, each of the university's planning units (college, school, and vice-presidential areas) was challenged to describe its specific strategies for carrying out these goals. These unit strategies were then reviewed at the institutional level, and judgments were made regarding priorities for action.

The basic planning organization of the University of Montana involves the University Planning Council (UPC), composed of members of constituent groups, faculty, staff, students, and administrators, who are asked to assume an institutional perspective rather than simply representing their constituents' interests. The UPC serves as an advisory council to the president. The UPC is given a series of charges: to critique the planning process and its schedule; to review planning assumptions, estimates of future resources, and other planning data; to review plans and resource requests from planning units and recommend priority issues for attention; and to present the results of its final deliberations as a series of formal recommendations to the president.

Each major academic and administrative unit of the university is designated as a planning unit. Each vice-president or dean serves as a unit head, responsible for coordinating program planning and budgeting for the unit. The role of unit heads has evolved gradually over the five planning cycles. In addition to being spokespersons for the aspirations and specific objectives of individual planning units, unit heads now serve as strategic advisors to the institution, meeting in joint session with the UPC.

The vice-president for academic affairs serves as the chief planning officer for the institution. He is responsible for the overall direction of the planning process, which includes coordination of weekly meetings with the UPC and unit heads, publication of an annual planning document, direction of the planning process throughout the year, and development of a series of final planning recommendations, which are presented to the president.

Each planning cycle begins with a review of the previous cycles and with the development of a plan of action for the coming year. This action plan is set within the context of the major themes and strategic priorities of the institution. Development of a correlative budget plan involves a thorough review of staffing patterns, equipment allocations, intermediate and long-range physical developments, legislative priorities, and private fundraising goals, as well as the distribution of a strategic investment pool of between 1 and 2 percent of the university's operating budget.

The UPC, in concert with the unit heads, presents a priority list of resource recommendations to the president in May of each year. The president in turn issues an annual planning report, communicating the set of resource allocation and reallocation decisions made by the president and major officers of the institution.

General Education and the Planning-Budgeting Process

The general education program provides an exemplary case study of the implementation of the planning-budgeting process at the University of Montana. In the late 1960s and early 1970s, the university followed the general pattern of American higher education institutions by abandoning core general education requirements in favor of broadly flexible curricular designs for individual students. In the late 1970s, a loosely defined distribution system involving more than seven hundred courses was adopted by the faculty and administration as a compromise position. Because the boundaries of course requirements in that system were so vague, the general education experience remained a relatively insignificant affair for most undergraduates. Subsequent efforts at general education reform by a dedicated group of faculty members were met either with indifference or resigned acceptance of the status quo by the majority of faculty members and administrators.

In 1981, a new president of the university articulated the need for general education reform. A refinement and expansion of that statement became the first theme of a set of fourteen major themes for the 1980s.

The University of Montana community identifies and supports, as the cornerstone of its educational mission, experiences that provide its students with knowledge and skills that are the essence of a liberal education. To this end, the university is committed to further development of the general education program for all undergraduate degree students, which will stimulate them to develop the capacity for written, oral and mathematical communications; to experience a wide scope of fields of knowledge; to appreciate critically their own culture and behavior, as well as the cultures and behaviors of others; to make sound and informed value judgments; and to think effectively and integrate knowledge (Bucklew, 1982, p. 18).

During that first planning cycle, the small group of faculty members who had worked on general education prior to 1981 were re-energized, and their cause was given institutional legitimacy through the planning process. The UPC assigned the highest priority ranking to a proposal submitted by the group through the college of arts and sciences. That proposal requested a modest investment from the planning enhancement pool of resources for faculty release time. That decision allowed those faculty members to be joined by administrators and students and to be constituted formally as the general education committee, with a specific institutional charge: to develop a comprehensive general education program for all undergraduate students.

During the 1982-83 planning cycle, the committee refined the concept of a comprehensive general education program and worked extensively with faculty members throughout the university to develop the curricular components of the program. In the summer of 1983, members of the committee and the vice-president for academic affairs participated in the Lilly Foundation Workshop in Colorado Springs. In that setting, they were able to explore various models of general education with colleagues from throughout the nation. In the fall of 1983, the president commissioned a member of the committee to draft a strategic planning report on the general education project. The report included specific implementation information on the program developed by the committee. In March of 1984 the president issued a set of strategic guidelines for planning, (Bucklew, 1984) which incorporated the findings of the report and outlined specific stages of implementating the program throughout the institution for the next five years.

With the advice of the UPC, and after consultation with the faculty senate, the president announced a set of major resource decisions to implement the general education program. These decisions included base and one-time-only resources from the enhancement pool and supplementary resources from donations to the university foundation.

The faculty senate approved the general education program in May of 1984 and worked with the president to begin implementation in the fall quarter of that year with the entering freshman class. That program includes competency requirements in writing, mathematics, foreign languages, and symbolic systems. It includes distribution requirements in six major perspectives: expressive arts, literary and artistic studies, historical and cultural studies in Western and non-Western traditions, social sciences, natural sciences, and ethics and human values. The program concludes with an integrative experience at the senior level, through a series of capstone courses.

Evaluation of the general education program at various stages after implementation will generate information about the strengths and weaknesses of the program and the relative success of its integration into the full range of undergraduate majors. Even at this early stage of implementation, however, the program can be judged as a successful example of institutional implementation of a planning-budgeting system.

What Works and Does Not Work

The cumulative experience of several institutions of higher education over the last few years has yielded a series of clues about what works and does not work in planning. The following list may be a helpful guide to what does not work in establishing a viable planning-budgeting process in institutions of higher education:
- Planning disconnected from the decision-making process of the institution
- Hearings or various public forum processes
- Reliance on committees for major decisions (planning ought to remain an advisory process designed to guide and influence the major decisions of the institution
- Reliance on committees for reduction or retrenchment efforts (it is important for committees to critique such efforts but not to create specific plans)
- Planning delegated primarily to a staff planning office.

A guide to what does work must include the following points:

1. A process that is described in understandable, written form and communicated to the campus community by the president or chancellor of the institution. This description should include a clear statement of major themes or goals and a practical framework for planning, which includes schedules, planning assumptions, strategic information, and assignment of responsibilities.

2. A process that is comprehensive (no segment of the institution should be exempted from participation).

3. A process that involves long-term (at least three to five years) strategic considerations, as well as annual budgeting decisions.

4. A process that combines bottom-up ideas and aspirations with broad institutional themes and priorities.

5. A process that requires presidential leadership and involvement. This includes the articulation of themes and priorities and commitment of time throughout the process—to monitor the activity of the planning council, to receive the council's recommendations, to make a series of decisions based on those recommendations, and to communicate the results to the campus community and relevant external constituencies.

The integration of a planning-budgeting process into the fabric of an institution's decision making is one of the more important challenges facing universities and colleges.

References

Bucklew, N. S. *University of Montana Framework for Planning.* Missoula: University of Montana, 1982.

Bucklew, N. S. *Strategic Guidelines for Planning.* Missoula: University of Montana, 1984.

Neil S. Bucklew is president of the University of Montana.

Daniel J. Smith is executive assistant to the president at the University of Montana.

A Western business school responds to external opportunities and threats with a comprehensive action plan. Key to its success is full participation by all constituencies.

Looking to the Future: Implementation of a Five-Year Plan

Phillip L. Beukema

The winter of 1983 was a pivotal time for the business school at Eastern Washington University. It was not the only such time in the school's fifteen-year history, but it was definitely a crucial point from the perspective of implementing what became known as the school's five-year development plan.

Rather than dealing with the substance of that development plan, this chapter focuses on the process involved in formulating the plan, as well as on the strategies pursued in implementing it. What is presented here is a case study of how one particular school met a series of challenges in undertaking those activities.

Why a Development Plan?

The simplest answer to this question is that the time was ripe. There was no comprehensive road map in place to which the faculty and administration of the business school could look for direction. The school was bordering on a state of drift, and the decision making function was predominantly passive.

Beyond the fact that no road map existed, a number of events were taking shape that could and in some cases would have serious implications for the business school. Eastern, as part of Washington's public higher education system, had sustained a series of budget cuts in the early 1980s, and in the fall of 1983 we were facing the prospect of further downward adjustments. The business school, of course, was regularly having to absorb its fair share of the reductions. Of no particular help was the fact that enrollment pressures were mounting, and the 1982-83 academic year was projected to bring the largest enrollment ever to the school. Since no funds were available for increasing the size of the faculty, the solution was to increase class sizes. If this was not enough, a full-scale merit system was to be installed that year, a first for the university. Given the controversy surrounding its adoption, it was certain that a good deal of careful attention would need to be paid to the entire process of implementing the plan. Additionally, the regional business community had for some time been expressing interest in having the school develop certain new programs and further extend its research and information services to the region. At that particular juncture, in fact, the school had been operating with a fairly stable set of degree programs, providing roughly the same menu for more than ten years.

One other factor also needs mention. An accredited member of the American Assembly of Collegiate Schools of Business (AACSB), Eastern's business school must regularly evaluate its programs and continually strive toward maintaining a set of quality academic programs that are conceptually and technologically up to date. As higher education moved into the 1980s, two areas in particular demanded an increasingly stronger and higher level of responsiveness on the part of business schools: microcomputer technology and international business. Prior to 1983, there was no clear sense of direction as to what kind of action should be taken to prepare our own school's graduates more effectively for meeting the real-world challenge of the computer and of the international context of business activity.

It was against this backdrop, then, that the need for a comprehensive, long-range strategic plan was perceived in mid-1982. No such plan was then in place; the budget was lean and looking even leaner; enrollment pressures were mounting; the system for evaluating and rewarding faculty performance was undergoing radical change; new program opportunities in the community were surfacing; and the curriculum was in need of reassessment and upgrading. Any one of these factors by itself could well have provided at least some rationale for engaging in a major planning effort; but, taken collectively, these events represented an urgent call for a concerted planning endeavor.

Formulating the Plan

The preparation, implementation, and subsequent monitoring of the five-year plan did not follow an orderly sequence of events. Not surprisingly, there were occasional delays, missteps, and unanticipated hurdles. Nevertheless, the entire process, from its inception up to the present time, has followed a course that has had a certain conscious order.

For expository purposes, the remainder of this chapter will be organized according to the sequence in which various planning stages occurred: (1) the planning process—who was involved, and how the process was accomplished; (2) internal implementation phase—refining objectives, modifying organizational structure, and developing new policies and programs; (3) external implementation phase—communication strategy and establishing support mechanisms; and (4) evaluation and follow-up planning—monitoring progress toward objectives and revising the plan. Each of these will be taken up in turn, beginning with a brief discussion of the planning process, as it took shape.

Events and circumstances surrounding the genesis of the school's development plan were perceived, with varying degrees of clarity, by a number of the school's faculty and administration, and to some extent by the school's external advisory board. Everyone recognized that there were a number of challenges and constraints and that a "policy" of continuing drift would not serve the students or faculty of the school.

Recognizing the pressing need for taking a deliberative approach to tackling the whole range of programmatic and resource challenges, we decided to confront the matter head-on. Specifically, the dean and staff of the school agreed to devote a full day to a faculty retreat. This retreat was to involve several small-group discussion sessions, each focusing on various aspects of the school's history, market environment, resource mix, and the like.

One very important feature of this retreat was the participation of the external advisory board, the Business Advisory Council. Earlier, it had been agreed that the council could and should play a key role in the retreat. Collectively, the council members possessed tremendous insight into external market and resource potentials. Equally important, though, was the need for faculty and council interaction and the important perceptions that would result from including the council very early in the whole planning and development process.

Thus, with a high level of faculty and council representation, discussions took place that formed the foundation of numerous follow-up work sessions. While the retreat did not by itself produce full-fledged solutions, it did yield a diversity of opinion and some common views. It generated useful perspectives on the school's challenges and constraints, and it provided some recommendations for action.

Immediately after the retreat, a planning task force was constituted, with representation from the academic departments of the school and from the administrative staff. This task force was charged with reviewing the various discussion summaries from the retreat, doing additional research as appropriate, and drafting a preliminary action plan for the school. This plan included a revised mission statement, new objectives touching on every aspect of the school's organization and operation, timeliness for implementation, a five-year budget for each category of objectives, and projections of personnel resources needed to accomplish certain sets of objectives. Little mention was made, at this juncture, of just where the resources would be obtained.

A working draft of the development plan was taken to a committee of the council for their review. This resulted in several refinements to the draft and tentative approval of the full plan. The draft, in turn, was taken back to the task force, where it was approved.

Three important steps were then taken in the planning process. First, a working draft of the plan was brought before the full faculty of the school for their comment. Following two faculty meetings and much discussion, a slightly modified version of the council's approved draft was unanimously accepted by the faculty. The second step was to take this new version back to the council. As might be expected, the council gave the plan its endorsement, urging the dean to take the plan to the university administration for its approval as well. The third step in the process was an indispensable element in the strategy of building a solid support base for the plan. This step involved presenting the plan, in its final form, to both the president and academic vice-president of the university for their endorsement. A brief discussion with these key individuals resulted in what can best be described as approval, without a specific commitment for personnel and budget.

Hence, in the winter of 1983, a comprehensive, long-range plan of development was ready for implementation. It was a plan of quality enhancement for what was already a good school. It provided new or improved educational services, called for a new organizational structure and new and greater resources, and responded realistically to an entire range of internal and external conditions, all of which were tied to the well-being of present and future students and faculty.

With the full support of the school's faculty, endorsement by the Business Advisory Council, and approval from the university administration, the stage was set for moving ahead with the five-year plan. No one was naïve enough to believe that the entire plan could be implemented without problems, nor did anyone suggest that the plan was doomed to failure because of the unlikely prospect of securing all the resources necessary to fulfill every new objective. There were some problems, but not many. Most important, the support and prior involvement of so many key personnel meant the plan had a good chance of succeeding.

Internal Implementation

The five-year plan detailed more than thirty objectives dealing with undergraduate and graduate programs, academic-community interface, faculty professional development, ancillary programs, public relations, and organization structure. In the weeks and months following the school's adoption of the plan, specific assignments were made to the departments and committees of the school to focus on objectives relevant to their scope of interest. Only objectives slated for implementation during the first eighteen months were considered at this stage.

A wide range of discussions and activities comprised this phase. In nearly all cases, the attempt was to delineate a particular objective, which had been stated briefly or in summary fashion within the planning document. Final recommendations on curricular changes or new policies were forwarded from the departments, either to the school's curriculum committee or to the administrative staff, as appropriate. The curriculum committee had responsibility for grappling with certain matters having schoolwide impact or implication. Recommendations from this committee were subsequently reviewed by the dean and his administrative staff prior to approval and follow-up action.

It must be emphasized that the objectives presented in the development plan were put forth as preliminary recommendations. Although the plan as a whole had wide support, the support was largely conceptual, in agreement with the general thrust but not necessarily with the particulars. There was no intention at the outset of the implementation process, therefore, that the document be a ready-made action plan; there was every expectation that a good deal of research and discussion take place. The testing of ideas, the refinement of certain objectives, the "selling" of certain courses—all of this needed to take place in a fairly free-flowing, back-and-forth process between and among various departments, committees, or councils. Nothing was given final approval unless it had been worked through the system, tested, and agreed to by the individuals or groups concerned and bore a mark of ownership by them.

Occasionally, the school's administrative staff concluded that a particular recommendation, and the consequences of its implementation, were of such magnitude that it should be taken before the entire faculty for final review and adoption. A proposed major change in the school's admissions and graduation standards was a case in point. In such instances, a draft proposal was also taken to the Business Advisory Council for its review.

Throughout the internal implementation phase, there were occasional behind-the-scenes efforts in which the dean communicated to the academic vice-president progress reports on results of the implementation activity and periodically requested special budget support for those elements of the plan that had originally been targeted for enlisting public (state) budgetary support. Funding for equipment and faculty positions are two prime examples of this type of support.

External Implementation

With several facets of the internal implementation effort under way, attention was directed to shaping the external dimension, the process and structure for securing the private funding and other support necessary for achieving the school's development objectives.

The earliest step taken was the decision to publish a quarterly newsletter, designed to communicate to our own alumni and business constituency a wide range of news items regarding the school. If we were to have long-range success in cultivating strong support from the business community and alumni, we had to develop a regular program of communication. Our supporters-to-be needed to know what the faculty and administration wanted to accomplish. They needed to be kept up to date regarding our faculty's achievements, activities of the professional student organizations and a whole range of efforts that were part of the ongoing process of implementing the five-year plan.

It seemed obvious to all of us then, and it still does today, that we would neither expect nor deserve the friendship and financial support of our external constituencies without being in regular communication with them as to our concerns, our aspirations, and our progress to date.

Following the initiation of the school's quarterly newsletter, we set about the task of creating a corporate support vehicle. From a good deal of research as to what had and had not been effective at a number of other professional schools in the country, a series of sequential decisions led to the concept of a corporate affiliate group. The Business Advisory Council was particularly instrumental in giving form and substance to this vehicle. Formally designated as the Corporate Associates Program, this support arm was established to help undergird the requirement for private resources, as spelled out in our development plan. The Corporate Associates Program is designed around the concept of an annual membership contribution, with the suggested size of contribution corresponding roughly to the size of the firm. For more than two years now, this group has served as the principal mechanism for generating a regular source of external financial support for enhancing the quality of the school's programs.

Once the Corporate Associates Program was established, the decision was made to form the school's own alumni chapter. By the end of 1983, a charter was developed, under the umbrella charter of the universitywide alumni organization, and the School of Business Alumni Advisory Board was formed. This board works with both the dean and the school's director for external relations to coordinate or spearhead activities designed to support the school. Internships, company visits, fundraising and placement assistance, and other avenues of support are becoming an increasingly larger factor in the school's total advancement effort. Alumni contributions have grown from less than 3 percent of the school's private-source income to more than 20 percent in two years.

Monitoring Results and Reinitiating the Cycle

As various aspects of the development plan were developed and implemented, the dean and selected committees monitored the ongoing activities and results. Within three years of the five-year plan's launching, at least 75 percent of its component objectives were either set in motion or accomplished. The success of the plan's implementation to date has been greatly aided by a combination of public and private funding. Throughout the university, public resource allocations provided for both computer facilities and faculty positions. Private funding, primarily from alumni and the corporate community, has provided significant support in such areas as program research and development, faculty professional development, and student services.

In the normal course of events, certain objectives established nearly three years ago are no longer appropriate. New opportunities have surfaced in the regional community. Budget and enrollment levels have changed, new faculty interests or concerns have become prominent, and many objectives already achieved under the development plan to date have prompted the need for a new planning cycle.

This cycle included several forums during 1985. Two formal sessions were held with department chairmen and faculty representatives, comprising a special-purpose task force. There have been meetings of the faculty and the school's administrative staff, as well as a variety of informal meetings involving individual and small groups of faculty. A faculty retreat held during the fall term of 1985 served as an additional forum for exploring a revised set of priorities and a new slate of objectives. Several staff meetings following the fall retreat served the purpose of finalizing a revised development plan.

With this revised road map in place, the school's planning activity came full circle, and the faculty and administration were ready to move into the 1986 calendar year with a new set of challenges.

A Final Word

The path to successful implementation was definitely not as smooth as this case study might suggest. There were missteps and false starts, and there was more than one occasion when, after a few months of unproductive discussion, it was necessary to regroup and start off on a new direction. On balance, however, the development plan provided a highly useful reference point. The process of implementation was greatly aided by an environment of strong support from school faculty, university administration, the Business Advisory Council, and the community at large.

Implementation of the plan has included some problems, but the prevailing pattern has been one of effective timing and results. Unquestionably, credit for success of the plan goes largely to the genuine involvement of all participants, both inside and outside the business school, both at the outset of the planning process and at a number of critical junctures throughout. These participants had at least some stake in one or more outcomes of the development plan, and they all had multiple opportunities to gain substantial ownership of the plan by the time it was finalized.

Further, successful implementation of the plan was almost automatically ensured by grounding it in the design phase. The planning process involved not only content planning but also planning of the implementation phase. This made it possible for a good deal of the implementation activity to begin well in advance of the time that the development plan was finalized. Thus, with a planning process that included a strong and consistent level of participation and an interweaving of both implementation and content planning, the results were fairly predictable. People who had a stake in the final outcome were fully involved in formulating the plan. People who were ultimately in the position either to grant or to withhold support from the entire endeavor granted it. The ongoing communication process continues to inform the school's constituencies about progress toward meeting development goals and, in turn, to enlist their continuing support for enhancing the quality of the school's educational services.

Phillip L. Beukema is dean of the School of Business at Eastern Washington University, with campuses in Spokane and Cheney, Washington.

Creating a new professional school is not a threat to the campus. It is a source of additional prestige and resources for all academic disciplines involved in the general education of the student.

The Professional School Concept: Breaking New Ground

Henry R. Anderson

Every professional school must break new ground. Such a concept normally takes several decades to evolve. Many forces work against the formation of a professional school. Universities in the forefront of each professional school movement must suffer from criticism originating at sister institutions. The purpose of this chapter is to elucidate the reasons for establishing a professional school and some of the difficulties faced by universities trying to phase in these schools. Of course, each different type of professional school faces different implementation problems. To illustrate the difficulty of establishing a separate professional school, the history of the formation of medical schools will be reviewed first. Second, an emerging professional school will be identified.

Continuing into the problems of professional school implementation, current barriers restricting or hindering the creation of such schools will be analyzed. These barriers usually consist of the university administration, faculty, resource allocation questions and beliefs, lack of early support by the profession's practitioners, and educating the public, since most universities are supported by public funds. The review of these barriers will be followed by an analysis of the costs and benefits associated with the creation of a professional school. Finally, focus will be directed to the future of the professional school movement.

What Is a Professional School?

A professional school houses an academic discipline that is closely connected with a recognized profession and is created in response to rigid educational requirements imposed upon a discipline by state laws and/or by a powerful national organization composed of practitioners. To qualify as a profession, the academic discipline must represent an occupation or a vocation that requires training in the liberal arts or in the sciences and advanced study in a specialized field. In addition, a minimum level of competence must be demonstrated before one is licensed to practice. The level of competence is measured in a number of ways, but if the public good is involved, licensing usually follows passage of state or national examinations. Since these professional disciplines are by their nature dynamic, practitioners are usually required to show proof of continuing educational activities after graduation in order to maintain licenses to practice. Schools of medicine and law are the most common professional schools on university campuses today.

When Should an Academic Discipline be Restructured into a Professional School?

The primary argument for establishing professional schools is the desire to provide more visibility and professional identity to an educational program. Such schools enhance professional identification on the part of students and lay the foundation for developing professional attitudes and ethics. The establishment of a professional school, in turn, gives the profession increased identity, which augments its stature in the eyes of the public. Professional schools make it possible to improve the scope and quality of education and provide opportunities for students to specialize in specific areas of professions.

Since, by definition, a profession requires advanced study in an appropriate discipline, control of curriculum is very important to defending the need for a separate, autonomous school. The critical issue is whether the present organizational structure provides the freedom and flexibility necessary to prepare well-educated people for their professional endeavors. The discipline must prepare its students for a specific vocation, and minimum state or national requirements must be met. The academic unit is answerable to its state-imposed requirements as much as it is to the university as a whole. If curriculum additions and changes can take place only after being scrutinized by collegewide committees, and if college constraints take precedence over the profession's requirements, then a traditional departmental structure is ineffective, and separate school status is needed.

As will be shown later in this chapter, a profession matures only after a strong national organization determines minimum educational requirements and strong professional schools implement those standards. Professional schools can move more quickly because their faculties can restructure curricula and change student admissions standards without constraints from other disciplines.

Emerging Professional Schools

In addition to the medical and law schools on campuses, several other disciplines are seeking school status. Some are just beginning their ascent to this plateau, while others are almost there. The engineering discipline is very close to gaining professional school status throughout the country. On many campuses, engineering is a college, while a few campuses still house engineering with other disciplines, such as the sciences. With the push toward high-tech supremacy, schools of engineering will become commonplace at our universities.

Accountancy is also emerging as a professional school. There already exists a national Federation of Schools of Accountancy. Currently, twenty-eight schools are members. The accounting profession is still struggling with the idea of a five-year degree program. Until this issue is resolved, the school concept will have secondary status. When the accounting profession comes out strongly in favor of a five-year education requirement, schools of accountancy will be created on every major university campus. Such schools will be needed to implement the five-year program. Other programs that are seeking school status are nursing and health. Both programs are just beginning to be recognized as independent disciplines, worthy of school status.

The Development of the Medical School

The medical profession dates back several centuries, and yet medical schools did not come into being in the United States until the 1800s. Even then, quality was not a part of the medical school movement. These schools, numbering more than seventy, were proprietary and free from university constraints. When additional difficulty was introduced into the curricula at one or two of the schools, students transferred to less rigorous schools. In fact, most schools advertised their programs in terms of short sessions and ease of progression (Kaufman, 1976).

The first regulation to restrict the practice of medicine was enacted in 1760 and was applicable only to the New York City area, yet no formal education of physicians was required for decades. Most early doctors served an apprenticeship with a preceptor. These preceptors were usually specialists who did not keep up with extensions in medical knowledge, and so the apprentice did not gain exposure to all general knowledge in the medical field. Between 1770 and 1810, academic standards of medical doctors were actually reduced because students lived in rural areas and could not afford the luxury of formal education. Major universities, such as Pennsylvania and Harvard, reduced requirements to attract students.

In the early 1800s, several medical schools were established, but they were proprietary in nature, even when they were connected with universities. During the first half of the nineteenth century, not much progress was made in increasing the educational requirements of physicians. Slowly, the prerequisite of a bachelor's degree evolved, but the medical profession remained far behind the other disciplines. In 1850-51, 80 percent of theology students and sixty-five percent of law students held bachelor of arts degrees, while only 20 percent of medical students had the same background (Kaufman, 1976).

The last half of the nineteenth century found major improvements being made in medical education. Strong European medical programs helped to improve the quality of medical education in the United States. American doctors educated in Europe returned to form medical schools at Johns Hopkins, Harvard, Western Reserve, and the University of California. Research centers at these and other leading universities significantly expanded the body of knowledge in medicine, which in turn caused the need for more advanced study and specialization. The creation of professional schools of medicine was the obvious solution to the need for increased competence of our medical doctors. Expansion of the common body of knowledge and increased dependence on specialization were the underlying factors. Since the turn of the century, the medical profession has come a long way, considering that bloodletting was a part of the curriculum as recently as 1870 (Kaufman, 1976).

Barriers to a New Academic Concept

To most people on a university campus, the frustrations of faculty members trying to implement new professional schools are either unknown or misunderstood. Much of the apparent lack of concern stems from a poor job of marketing on the part of the faculty of the fledgling professional school. However, there also exists a high level of animosity on the part of administrators and faculty from other disciplines. Part of this open enmity is caused by the faculty of the professional school failing to communicate the benefits that would be derived by the campus if such a school were created. In order to implement a new professional school, its faculty must understand the hurdles to be overcome and develop a strategic plan to scale these apparent obstacles.

University Administrators

University administrators hold the key to the implementation of a professional school, and yet most are unaware of the plight of the aspiring discipline. Several reasons can be identified: (1) Most universities operate with several layers of administrators, and it is very difficult to get an original idea exposed to the academic vice-president or the president on a timely basis. (2) Most university administrations are ruled by nonprofession-oriented faculty, and they tend to resist having another professional school rise within their midst. (3) Even if the idea of creating a professional school does penetrate the administrative armor, it normally is not given high priority for consideration. Resource implications are usually given as the reason for rejecting the concept.

What is needed is a full-scale plan of communication with the central administration. A knowledge of campus politics is essential. The plan should include a well-developed program for increasing total campus financial contributions from area practitioners and alumni. Total campus benefits are linked to the success of the professional school movement.

Other Administrators and Faculty

Linked closely with the lack of response of the university administration is the lack of excitement on the part of the chief school administrator, in most cases the dean. Any unit that is considering becoming an autonomous school must be a mature, contributing department of an organized school or college. Such a unit has high demand for its courses and usually high enrollments. Resources are linked directly to student credit hours, and so the creation of a new school threatens the resource allocation of the college. Deans are also aware of possible cuts in their outside funding that can occur when a new school is developed.

College faculty today are very resource-conscious. Any change that threatens existing resources invites a negative response. The fact that the new school represents an important step for the university and its student body is usually a moot point. Resource reductions are life-threatening. In addition, many faculty members are unaware of the identity of the profession behind the movement. They believe that the discipline has been an integral part of the college for many years and should remain so.

Again, the main issue is one of communication. However, strong support from the private sector provides considerable assistance in convincing the dean and the college's faculty of the merits of the new school.

Slow Response from the Profession

One of the biggest frustrations in a move to create a professional school is the long time gap between the profession's national organization identifying the need for and placing high priority on the establishment of such schools and the national, statewide, and local offices of the profession's practitioners becoming aware of the need for the movement and lending their support to the school's faculty. Such support carries much weight when the faculty is trying to convince the administration of the need for the change in status. Most local offices are busy with their day-to-day tasks and are not informed by the national organization on a regular basis. Even when they are informed, the national office often fails to get the message across. It usually takes years to change an academic doctrine, and failure of the profession's practitioners to keep abreast of pending academic changes is one of the main reasons for this delay. The solution, as before, is to build a strong case for the change and then make sure the facts are communicated to practitioners.

Educating the Public

Public acceptance of the concept of a professional school is also very important. Most major universities are state-supported institutions. The public generally does not understand or care to understand the workings of the administration of a university, but the citizenry is often vocal when resources appear to be wasted. The public can also play an important part in the creation of a professional school. As was stated earlier, professional schools are developed to serve some segment of the population, whether through medicine, law, or accountancy. If the public feels that through the creation of such a school the public will be better served by the university, then the public will support such a move. If the proposed school's faculty can make a strong case to the community, illustrating how the new school will eliminate the threat of some public wrongdoings, then the administration will be hard-pressed not to allow the creation of the school. Therefore, the public needs to be continuously informed of the direction and purpose of the proposed school.

State legislatures and boards of regents are often involved in decisions to create professional schools. Here, again, there is a need for the development of a strong case backing the need for the school. Universities in the same state system should work together to inform regents and legislators of the benefit of the new school to the state and its citizens. Only such joint efforts will work in a multicampus system.

Cost-Benefit Analysis for a New Professional School

Cost-benefit analysis for the purpose of establishing a new professional school differs from similar analyses in industry. In most university-related cases, it is not enough to simply show that benefits outweigh costs. This is not to say that such analysis is not important, but creating a new operating segment on campus is a major move. New administrative and faculty positions are required. New support staff positions usually accompany increases in administrative and faculty positions. The resource allocation process for the entire campus is going to be changed. This means that each existing operating segment, whether a department, a support function, or a student organization, will be affected by this change. Therefore, it is extremely important that the cost-benefit study clearly show benefits to outweigh costs.

The cost side of the analysis has already begun in our discussion. New positions and related benefit packages are expensive and will require either new financial resources or a reallocation of existing dollars. Neither of these alternatives will be well received by other faculty members on a campus. Additional costs may include new facilities, change-over for the college in which the school used to be housed, reprinting of stationery, new diplomas and possible graduation ceremonies, and a redistribution of capital equipment dollars.

Benefits are a bit more difficult to perceive. Most proposed professional school programs would identify all or most of the following benefits:
1. Curriculum changes can be made that satisfy the demands of the profession without opposition from people outside the profession.
2. The new school raises the visibility of the university because it is seen as being on the cutting edge of educational endeavors.
3. Professional schools operate more efficiently than their predecessor departments because of less duplication of effort and less resistance to professional pressures.
4. Creation of the new school identifies the campus as part of a national movement.
5. The morale of the school's faculty will be increased because of closer association with the profession.
6. Increased outside financial support usually accompanies the formation of a new professional school.
7. Faculty recruiting efforts will be enhanced.
8. Students will have a closer association with and appreciation for the profession.

Do the benefits outweigh the costs? Since most of the benefits are not quantifiable, it is very difficult to determine with any precision which side to favor. However, because of the major campus changes resulting from the new school, few would agree that the benefits identified above would justify the change. There would be just too much chaos to suffer through for benefits that are at best speculative.

Developing a Strategic Plan

In order to build a convincing case, the new school must identify an overriding, unique benefit that by itself justifies the change. The new school must improve society in some way. The new school must be able to do some things better than its predecessor organization did.

The profession associated with the school has usually grown to such a point that its common body of knowledge no longer fits nto the normal four-year format. The profession is usually encountering some problems, and correcting them becomes a primary issue. These problems must be solved for the betterment of the public. Specialization is necessary, and different teaching and learning patterns must be developed. Unique, specially tailored seminars must be created. At this point in the master plan, these problems of the profession should be highlighted and discussed. Examples include lawsuits resulting from unethical practices, unacceptable conclusions drawn by practitioners resulting in harm to the public, cases of practitioner fraud, and cases of general incompetence of practitioners.

Problem identification should be followed by a specific outline of ways that the proposed new professional school would help eliminate these problem areas. A strong case should be made that the graduate would be better prepared to face the difficulties of the profession after experiencing the proposed curriculum and structure of the new school. The increased qualifications of the graduates should be connected with specific advanced coursework designed for that primary purpose.

The faculty of professional schools have significantly more flexibility in changing curricula to satisfy the needs of the profession. Responsiveness and creativity are augmented by school status. Professions, as mentioned earlier, require special, advanced, fifth-year coursework, and professional schools enhance these offerings.

The task of preparing a strategic plan is made significantly easier if the profession's national organization has developed a strong position in favor of professional schools, created a plan to communicate its opinion to all major universities and colleges, and identified methods of convincing practitioners to support local university movements. If the profession does not openly support the concept, individual professional programs will find it extremely difficult to convince university administrators and faculty that the professional school is necessary.

Breaking New Ground

Professions experience significant increases in their common bodies of knowledge as they mature. In addition, problems in practice highlight inadequacies in the profession's academic preparation. These two factors point to a need for expansion of the academic program beyond the usual four-year curriculum. As new types of courses are developed, and as five- and six-year degree programs are implemented, specialization occurs. At this point, administration of the professional discipline must change to cope with the unique demands of the profession. Creating a professional school is a good way to solve this problem.

Reference

Kaufman, M. *American Medical Education: Formative Years, 1765–1910*. Westport, Conn.: Greenwood Press, 1976.

Henry R. Anderson is director of the School of Accounting at the University of Central Florida and former dean of the School of Business Administration and Economics at California State University, Fullerton.

The use of information management strategies by chief academic managers has become an absolute necessity for the competitive edge.

Implementing Information Management Strategies

C. E. Tapie Rohm, Jr., Pat McInturff, Hal Hoverland

Academic institutions are undergoing an extraordinary metamorphosis that is transforming them into competitive organizations in a dynamically changing society. This changing society is information-based and has been developing new rules and conditions, which many academic managers do not understand. No longer are yesterday's methods sufficient for today's conditions.

The exact nature of the metamorphosis is still not clearly understood. However, the transformation seems to be taking on added significance for academic managers to develop the competitive edge. The thrust of this chapter is to describe the new information society and strategies available to academic managers in this new environment. The preponderance of evidence indicates that our society is becoming an information society, which is segmented into three divisions of labor: the information worker, the information manager, and the information specialist. With this segmentation, new directions are being developed. The academic manager will need to implement new information management strategies in three areas: faculty development, curricular design, and administrative services. Implementing new information management strategies will develop a better competitive edge for the academic manager.

The Information Society

The information society was first introduced in the 1950s. Two significant dates, 1951 and 1956, are crucial for our understanding. In 1951, the first commercial computer was introduced to the workplace. With this introduction of the computer to the workplace, a whole new way of thinking was developed. No longer were people the main focus for achieving specific tasks. The notion of hiring more people to accomplish a specific task started to collapse. Specific tasks, especially the utilization of numerical data for finance, accounting, and statistical reporting, could be accomplished in a matter of hours instead of days, weeks, and months. The second date, 1956, was when the number of white-collar workers first outnumbered blue-collar workers. This emphasis moved us out of the blue-collar age, commonly referred to as the industrial society, into the initial stage of the information society.

The next significant period of the information society was the introduction of the personal computer. Although the first personal computer, based on microcomputer processor technology, was introduced in 1977, the year 1981 marks the official acceptance of the personal computer by IBM. The personal computers of today are the mainframe computers of yesteryear. The personal computer has started to permeate every facet of our lives. Thus, as this information society starts to gain significant momentum, divisions are becoming clearer.

The information worker is the new force of today and the future. This information worker is replacing the traditional worker in a variety of industries and professions. An information worker is any worker who utilizes or will utilize a computer to accomplish daily tasks. An information worker will be found everywhere in the workplace because the computer is evolving into a commonplace, everyday tool.

The computer is no longer used only for quantitative functions but is being used everywhere in the workplace because of its small size. Not only can computers do quantitative operations; their technology is also being utilized in such small appliances as toasters, blenders, and microwave ovens, in programmed power tools, computer-generated blueprints, energy-efficient thermostats, surveillance devices in the building industry, copiers, word processors, electronic mail-in office automation, in parts for the automotive industry, and for process control in manufacturing. New applications are being developed daily. An information worker is not a person who operates a computer but one who uses this technology to accomplish a prescribed task. This distinction seems small but will increase in the future.

The information manager is the person who manages information workers. This particular type of manager will play a leading role in the development of the information worker. The information manager will need certain skills and knowledge levels beyond those required by the information worker. These skills and knowledge levels, which include innovation, control, and participatory management, are necessary for the information manager to survive.

The information specialist is a professional in the information society, whose expertise exceeds that of the information worker and the information manager. Information specialists have been found traditionally in data processing centers. The data processing center has supplied operators, programmers, systems analysts, and often vendors, whose sales forces supply necessary equipment for workplaces. There are also consultants, whose knowledge and experience help to save time and money, and researchers, who continue to develop new technologies. The class of information specialists is continually increasing with advancing technology.

Academic Management

The traditional academic management hierarchy is usually represented with a president and two officers, whose roles are divided between the academic and administrative areas. The academic officer usually has responsibility for the faculty, students, and curricular programs. Faculty retention, tenure, promotion, and student concerns generally dominate this area, along with curricular design and development issues. The administrative officer spends a majority of time on physical facilities, fundraising, staff concerns, grants, and budgetary considerations. An executive council is usually formed to review all proposed decisions and make recommendations to the president.

With the advent of the information society, the traditional roles of academic managers are changing. The change is being fostered by the introduction of computerization into every part of the academic institution, thus necessitating new strategies.

Academic institutions can increase productivity and improve performance by implementing information management strategies in faculty development, curricular design, and administrative services.

Faculty Development

Faculty need to learn about the power of the computer by experiencing it. Too often, faculty have become intimidated by this technology and forgo learning about it. Some students acquire significant expertise on the personal computer, and this intimidates some faculty, to the extent that they avoid using computer applications in their courses. If faculty develpment programs included computer training, then a great amount of faculty fear and trepidation would dissipate. Faculty must adapt to the new information age by incorporating computers into their teaching and research.

Budgetary considerations represent a major obstacle for not supporting faculty with sufficient computerization. However, recent price reductions in the marketplace have helped to solve part of this problem. Two years ago, a typical personal computer, such as an IBM PC with two disk drives, monitor, and 256K of memory, would have cost approximately $3,500. Today, the same system can be purchased for $1,500 or less. If an academic institution opts for an IBM clone, the same system can be purchased for $500. Technological advances are constantly outdating current equipment, sometimes before it is even sold. Even though the equipment is technologically obsolete, this equipment is functionally operable. Thus, the quest for state-of-the-art equipment should not overshadow the need for action today.

Curricular Design

Incorporating the computer into curricular design will never become complete until faculty know and understand computers. The Massachusetts Institute of Technology's Sloan School of Management's recent experience emphasizes this point. The school provided personal computers for all interested faculty. The faculty then took a year to become familiar and comfortable with the equipment. During the process of learning how to use the personal computer, the faculty started to think of how they could implement various aspects of the personal computer into their teaching. As the faculty became proficient with their computers, curricular design changes started to appear. Now, nearly all courses include some aspect of computerization.

One might think that the greatest resistance to computerization of curricular design would come from the liberal arts. However, there is a trend for English departments to incorporate the computer into writing classes. The writing process is a thinking process, and the computer facilitates the mechanics of the process. Editing becomes easier for the student and produces better results. English writing classes that use computers are becoming very popular courses.

Analysis of an institution's curricula will reveal that a personal computer can be used to enhance every course offered. This is because every course can always use a personal computer to retrieve information from some sort of data base especially designed for the course, as well as to analyze various aspects of the course. The computer assists faculty members and students in doing tasks faster, more reliably, and accurately and in providing access to vast amounts of relevant information.

In our School of Business and Public Administration, we realized that our students needed to know more about the power of the computer. Students discover this by learning about the information tools. The information tools are represented by four areas: information processing, information forecasting, information-based management, and information problem solving.

Information processing consists of the student learning about word processing and graphics. A student who can use a word processing and graphics software package can produce better-looking reports in a relatively short period of time. The arduous task of rewriting a report becomes simpler and easier.

Information forecasting allows a student to manipulate financial and statistical data in a more sophisiticated and easier manner. When students learn how to use an electronic spreadsheet and various other interactive modeling packages, they are equipped with stronger analytical tools and are more likely to utilize them.

Information-based management is the use of data-based management software packages by students. When students master the concept of data-base management systems, they know how to structure the information storage and retrieval needs of a person or an organization. Information storage and retrieval allow a person to produce more relevant information about a given subject for decision making purposes and constitute an extremely powerful tool.

Information problem solving covers the areas of heuristics and algorithms. Heuristics helps a student to learn new ways of solving problems that are encountered in daily life. Algorithms look for systematic means to computerize any problem. Computer languages and mathematical methods are combined together to write new programs. New programs help generate new insights.

Administrative Services

The academic institution can realize added benefits from the information society. Although administrative services currently utilize computers in their activities, the complete power of the personal computer remains to be fully discovered.

The most obvious use of personal computers is in the clerical area. Replacing the typewriter with a personal computer and a printer invariably increases productivity. However, a transformation needs to take place. This transformation is the consolidation of the current technology. There is an information worker, a secretary, who has an IBM Selectric III typewriter, a computer terminal that is hardwired into the main computer, and an IBM PC-XT personal computer with a printer. The institution needs to remove the typewriter and computer terminal and use the personal computer with its printer as the typewriter and computer terminal. Reduction of old technology for such advanced technology as personal computers will save resources.

The use of personal computers, either as standalone units or hooked into the mainframe computer, can be accomplished by administrators and staff. An administrator can generate and track budget items by using an electronic spreadsheet. If the budget is hypothetically cut 10 percent, the effect on a variety of programs can be seen instantly.

Another use of the computer is in the "electronic file cabinet," which is a data-based management system. Data-based management packages, whether on the mainframe computer or on the personal computer, can save considerable time. What is even more important is that most individuals can set up a data-based management system, using software, in a much shorter period of time than was required in using the mainframe. The application of the information tools to administrative services will greatly enhance productivity and the quality of work life.

Conclusion

Chief academic officers need to become aware of the changes being produced by the new information society. With the evolution of this new society, new types of workers and managers are emerging. New skills and abilities need to be implemented at academic institutions, especially in academic management, to develop a competitive edge.

Academic managers must help faculty by supplying the necessary resources to develop faculty's confidence in using computers. After faculty have mastered the personal computer, curricular design changes will follow. The age of the information society has arrived. We need to master the technology.

C. E. Tapie Rohm, Jr., is director of information management programs in the School of Business and Public Administration at California State University, San Bernardino.

Pat McInturff is professor of management at California State University, San Bernardino.

Hal Hoverland is dean of the School of Business and Public Administration at California State University, San Bernardino.

Conclusion: Putting the Pieces Together

If for no other reason, this volume is important because it presents a candid appraisal of approaches used by selected academic administrators whose institutions have met numerous challenges during a very chaotic period. However, this volume contributes to the literature of academic management by presenting various tactics, insights, and strategies that have worked successfully. Obviously, there is no one unique, magical framework that solves all conflicts, balances the budget, and plans future strategies.

The reason that simple managerial decision trees and "cookbook" approaches to management have not regularly generated desired outcomes is probably the pervasive uncertainty that has been present during the 1970s and 1980s. This uncertainty has appeared in several segments of the academic experience, ranging from career choices by students to lack of security for senior professors. The uncertainty and chaos had the basic impact of altering nearly all the social, political, and economic bonds of the institution. Thus, the hallowed halls became at times a jungle, with self-interest and survival the basic goals.

Yet, despite this dismal portrait of American higher education, most insititutions did survive, although in many instances in very different forms, with new missions and altered political and economic alliances. Institutional survival can be attributed to a composite of various attributes. From the candid appraisal of those administrators presented in this volume, it would appear that the attributes most often suggested are very basic—leadership, creativity, the open-systems approach, and participatory management.

Leadership as a managerial concept has been greatly ignored in the management literature over the last several decades. But leadership has had a rejuvenation, as embodied by the turnaround of Chrysler by Lee Iacocca. With increased uncertainty, the charismatic leader becomes more important as a focus and rallying point of the organization. In higher education, with broadly set goals, the need for leadership takes on increased importance during times of chaos.

Creativity and innovation also are of increased importance during turbulent periods. The ability to break out of routines and formulate new missions and relationships becomes critical, especially when many of the old rules and assumptions of the institution lose their appeal. Higher education, like management in general, is witnessing a new focus on innovation and innovative organizations. Clearly, innovation and creativity were important attributes, necessary for the survival and at times even growth of academic institutions during the recent chaotic decade.

Another important attribute commonly cited by the commentators in this volume is viewing the organization as an open system. A great deal of managerial literature has amplified the importance and need for taking an open-systems approach. However, it is much easier to prescribe than implement. One reason is that an open-systems approach is very risky, because the organization is subject to a greater array of pressures and stimuli than in the protective posture of the closed system. By definition, the open system implies an increased number of variables that must be taken into account, which in turn means possibly more risk, as well as greater capability to identify and manipulate the increased number of possible decisional inputs.

Another feature of note in the candid comments of the commentators in this volume is that they viewed institutions as human systems with participatory management. Viewing the academic institution as not only an open system but also as a human system recognizes the importance of the human factor in the operations of an organization. By its very nature, the academic enterprise is labor-intensive. To omit people from the decision process and focus solely on budgets, capital items, and physical plant is to ignore a primary strength of the institution. Managers who are aware of people find an additional resource with which to counter the risks and uncertainty encountered in the open-systems approach.

The final attribute is a set of personal traits often ignored in the literature, but which often make a substantial difference in academic management. That difference is the manager's conviction and courage.

Index

A

Accountancy, 101
Alumni, as volunteers, 22-23
Anderson, H. R., 99, 107
Aristotle, 47
Arnold, M., 45-46, 52
Astin, A. W., 49, 52

B

Bankruptcy, 33
Barnett, S., 33, 41
Benefits: suggested employee, 77-78; of new professional school, 105
Berman, Weiler Associates, 28, 32
Beukema, P. L., 91, 98
Biemiler, L., 33, 41
Board of Governors, California Community Colleges, 27-28, 32
Bonds, tax-exempt, 20
Bothwell, L., 73, 77, 78, 79
Brigham Young University, 49-51
Bucklew, N. S., 83, 87, 89
Budgeting, 83; and academic management, 4-5; and planning, 58; process of planning and, 83-89
Budgets, analysis of, at public universities, 10, 13

C

California Community Colleges. *See* Board of Governors; Chancellor's Office; Community colleges
California Educational Facilities Act, 20
California Master Plan Commission, 27
CAMPUS (Campus Analytical Methods for Planning in University Systems), 34, 55, 59
Chancellor's Office, California Community Colleges, 32
Change: constraints to, 64; determining actual, 13; in higher education due to information technology, 109-114; institutional attitude toward, 14-15; mission statement as catalyst for, 48-49; Naisbitt's predictions on, 74-75
Coleman, J. W., 53, 61
Colleges. *See* Community colleges; Institutions, private; Institutions, public
Community colleges, Proposition 13 and California's, 25-32
Competition, 109
Computers, 74, 110; and administrative services, 113-114; and curriculum, 112-113; and faculty, 111-112
Conner, P. E., 64, 71
Constraints: characteristics of, 65; context and conditions of, 63-65; multiple complex, 70-71; removal process for, 66-70
CPA model. *See* Crisis Prevention Analysis (CPA) Model
Crisis Prevention Analysis (CPA) Model, 37; application of, 35, 38; concepts underlying, 38-40; conclusions regarding, 40-41; evaluation criteria of, 36
Cropxey, J., 47, 52
Culture: corporate, 75; and institutions of higher education, 45-48
Curriculum, and information technology, 112-113

D

Deal, T. E., 75, 76, 78
Decision making, 3; at California's community colleges, 31; in higher education, 5. *See also* Implementation; Problem identification; Solutions, search for
Drucker, P. F., 64, 71

E

Eastern Washington University's plan: conclusions on, 97-98; external

117

implementation of, 95-96; formulation of, 92-94; internal implementation of, 94-95; monitoring results of, 96-97; reason for development of, 91-92
Economics, and higher education, 4-5
Education, higher. See Higher education
EDUCOM-EFPM, 55, 59
Eisenhower College, 33
Emery, J. C., 59, 61
Employees, encouraging self-reliant, 76-78. See also Faculty; Personnel; Staff
Endowment, 19
Enrollment: analysis of, at public universities, 10-12
Excellence, qualities of organizations achieving, 75

F

Facilities, care of, at private institutions, 19-20
Faculty: and CPA model, 39; development and computers, 111-112; and new professional schools, 103
Federation of Schools of Accountancy, 101
Field Research Corporation, 32
Fundraising, 20

G

Government, financial aid to institutions by, 18
Greenwood, W. F., 71
Griswold, W., 45
Guzzardi, W., Jr., 51, 52

H

Harvard University, 102
Hayward, G. C., 25, 32
Higher education: changes in, due to information technology, 111-114; constituency of, 4; and culture, 45-48; decision making in, 5; economic environment of, 4-5; external environment of, 2-3; increasing competition in, 109; ironies of, 1-2; mission of, 3-4

Holland, J. R., 49, 52
Hopkins, D. S. P., 34, 41, 55, 60, 61
Hoverland, H., 5, 6, 33, 41, 109, 114

I

Iacocca, L., 115
Implementation, 81; of five-year plan at Eastern Washington University, 91-98; of information management strategies, 109-114; of new professional school, 99-106; of planning-budgeting process, 83-89
Information society, 110-111; administrative services in, 113-114; changes in academic management in, 111; curricular design in, 112-113; faculty development in, 111-112
Information systems: at California community colleges, 29-30
Institutions, private: fiscal responsibility at, 18-20; mission and purpose of, 20-21; resources for, 21-23
Institutions, public: analysis ratios for, 10-13; external pressures on, 9-10; recognizing problems as policy issues at, 13-16

J

James, W., 47
Jarvis, H., 26
Johns Hopkins University, 102

K

Kaufman, M., 101, 102, 106
Kennedy, A. A., 75, 76, 78

L

Landis, C. P., 59, 61
Lawrence, P. R., 71
Leadership, 25, 51, 115
Levine, A., 49, 52
Liberal arts, 3-4
Life planning programs, 77-78
Lindquist, J., 58, 61
Lorsch, J. W., 71

M

McInturff, P., 5, 6, 33, 41, 109, 114
Management: and budgeting, 4-5; challenges of educational, 73-74; changes in academic, due to information technology, 111; to encourage self-reliance and excellence, 76-78; enhancement of, 53-54; four phases of cycle of, 55-56, 58; suggested attributes for, 115-116
Massachusetts Institute of Technology's Sloan School of Management, 112
Massey, W. F., 34, 41, 55, 60, 61
Medical school, development of, 101-102
MIS (Management Information Systems), 59
Mission: of Brigham Young University, 49-51; of California's community colleges, 26-27; of higher education, 3-4; importance of statement of, 20-21; statement of, as catalyst for change, 48-49
Models, 61; planning and resource allocation, 58-60
Montana, University of: general education and planning-budgeting process of, 86-88; planning-budgeting process of, 84-86
Moore, D. R., 17, 23
Morgan, A., 54, 61
Mouritsen, M. M., 45, 52

N

Naisbitt, J., 74, 76, 78

O

O'Neill, J. P., 33, 41
Organizations, qualities of, with excellence, 75

P

Parker, R., 63, 66, 71, 72
Perry, R. B., 47, 52
Personnel, reduction in costs of, 19. See also Employees; Faculty; Staff
Peters, T. J., 75, 76, 78

Ping, C. J., 9, 16
Plan, five-year, implementation of, at Eastern Washington University, 91-98. See also Eastern Washington University's plan
Planning, 83; and budgeting, 58; at California's community colleges, 30-31; in management cycle, 55; and resource allocation models, 58-60
Planning-budgeting process: characteristics of effective, 83-84; general education and, 86-88; University of Montana's, 84-86; what does and does not work in, 88
Policy, defining problems as issues of, 13-16
Pomona College, 20
PPBS (Planning, Programming Budget System), 54, 59
Problem identification, 7; California community college examples of, 29-32; at community colleges, 29; Crisis Prevention Analysis Model for, 33-41; at public universities, 9-16; and stewardship of resources at private institutions, 17-23
Professional school(s): cost-benefit analysis for new, 104-105; definition of, 100; developing strategic plan for new, 105-106; development of medicine as, 101-102; educating public about new, 104; emerging, 101; profession and new, 103-104; time for establishing, 100-101; university administrators and new, 102-103
Proposition 13, 2; and California's community colleges, 25-32

R

Recruitment, using alumni for, 22
Redlands, University of: committee for trustee development at, 21-22; student loan program of, 18-19; volunteers at, 22-23
Resource(s): allocation models, 58-60; allocation strategies for, 54; for private institutions, 21-23; stewardship of, at private institutions, 18-20

RRPM (Resource Requirements Prediction Model), 34, 55, 59
Rudolph, F., 14, 16

S

Shaw College, 33
Smith, B. O., 65, 72
Smith, D. J., 83, 89
Solutions, search for, 43; constraint removal as, 63-71; human factor in, 73-78; mission statement's role in, 45-51; planning and resource allocation management as, 53-61
Space, analysis of, at public universities, 10, 12-13
Staff: analysis of, at public universities, 10, 12; and CPA model, 39
Strauss, L., 47, 52

T

Tapie Rohm, C. E., Jr., 5, 6, 33, 41, 109, 114
Tax(es): initiatives of 1970s, 2; after Proposition 13 and California's community colleges, 26; and public institutions, 9-10

TRADES, 55, 59
Trustees, as resource for private institutions, 21-22
Tuition: dependence on, 18

U

Universities. *See* Institutions, private; Institutions, public
University of California, 102

V

Valéry, P., 25
Values: at Brigham Young University, 49-51; and institutions of higher education, 46-48
Volunteers, as resource for private institutions, 22-23

W

Waterman, R. H., Jr., 75, 76, 78
Western Reserve University, 102
Westminster College, 33
Woodring, P., 46, 52
Wyatt, J. P., 59, 61